Pamela Smith does it again! From her excellent book on chakras (*Inner Drives*) to *The Power of the Dark Side* and now this wonderful resource on symbols, she has the gift of translating the esoteric into the practical. Practical tools for today — for writers, artists, and content creators wishing for a more conscious creativity to imbue deeper meaning in their work and creations. Bravo, Pamela! A must for everyone's library.

    Kate McCallum — Producer/Writer. Founder, c3: Center for Conscious Creativity

Pamela Jaye Smith's fascinating book on symbols and their meaning is a valuable tool for me as a life coach and practitioner of Oriental Medicine. Since profound changes in our lives and the rediscovery of balance and wellness are deeply rooted in the subconscious, a clear understanding of the origins of our myths and the ideas that support our most primary beliefs about ourselves and our actions are of infinite importance to unraveling the mystery of how and why our lives work.

    Geffrey von Gerlach — Licensed Acupuncturist, Life Coach

Effective use of imagery is essential to reach an audience with immediacy and depth. In *Symbols.Images.Codes*, Ms. Smith has decoded a vast number of such images and presented a virtual catalog of ideas and their potential uses for content creators, be it for movies, games, novels, plays, or marketing. It is a reference book that many will want to turn to time and time again to deepen and broaden the ways in which they drive the emotional intensity of their creations.

    Aurora Miller — Director, Digital Content, Panoramic Entertainment

Symbols.Images.Codes is a dynamic litmus test for writers and directors to examine their characters' behavior, actions, and appearance; a great tool for providing a rich subtext for storytelling in any genre.

    Robert R McGinley — Writer, Director, Photographer; *Jimmy Zip, Topography, Light and Magic*

With our youth focused on instantaneous gratification through TV, movies, video games and the Internet, they have become expert at communicating in the blink of an eye through the power of images. By plugging us into the transformative nature of symbols, images and codes, Ms. Smith has tapped the universal consciousness to reveal the hidden nature of this imagery, which can evoke memories and feelings, while motivating us to design new forms of language. This compelling book opens the door to stimulating discussion, brainstorming and fresh creativity. Every student and teacher should have a copy to use as a comprehensive reference tool, and to motivate them to develop as individuals and for the benefit of others.

    Jill Gurr — Founder and Exec Director, Create Now; Screenwriter

Packed with insights and explanations that inform the human condition and inspire the creative process, this book packs the wallop of a scholarly reference work (which it is), yet presents with the ease and pleasure of reading a novel. A gem with a permanent place on my bookshelf.

    Brian A. Wilson — Writer/Filmmaker

SYMBOLS · IMAGES · CODES

THE SECRET LANGUAGE OF MEANING IN FILM, TV, GAMES, AND VISUAL MEDIA

PAMELA JAYE SMITH

MICHAEL WIESE PRODUCTIONS

Published by Michael Wiese Productions
12400 Ventura Blvd. #1111
Studio City, CA 91604
(818) 379-8799, (818) 986-3408 (FAX)
mw@mwp.com
www.mwp.com

Cover design by MWP
Interior design by William Morosi
Edited by Bob Somerville
Printed by McNaughton & Gunn

Manufactured in the United States of America
Copyright 2010 by Pamela Jaye Smith

Library of Congress Cataloging-in-Publication Data

Smith, Pamela Jaye
 Symbols, images & codes : the secret language of meaning in film, tv, games and visual media
/ Pamela Jaye Smith.
      p. cm.
 Includes bibliographical references and index.
 ISBN 978-1-932907-74-2
1. Symbolism in mass media. 2. Visual communication. I. Title. II. Title: Symbols, images
and codes.
 P96.S96S65 2010
 302.23--dc22
                              2010001190

Printed on Recycled Stock

DEDICATION

To Georgia Lambert, wisdom teacher extraordinaire. She reveals in fascinating and enlightening ways the many levels of meaning in symbols, images, and codes, from the obvious to the obscure, as well as the formerly deeply secret.

And to Monty Hayes McMillan, a man of vision who taught me how to see the hidden meanings behind many things.

TABLE OF CONTENTS

ACKNOWLEDGMENTS . . . . *viii*

INTRODUCTION . . . .*ix*

HOW TO USE THIS BOOK . . . . *xii*

HOW SYMBOLS WORK . . . . *xv*

1. ASTRONOMY AND ASTROLOGY *1*

2. COMPOSITION *4*

3. NUMBERS *7*

4. CODES *11*

5. EARTH *15*

6. AIR *19*

7. FIRE *23*

8. WATER *27*

9. ANIMALS *32*

10. CHAKRAS *35*

11. COLOR *39*

12. THE LEAP *44*

13. ANATOMY *49*

14. CLOTHES *54*

15. ARCHITECTURE *65*

16. STEPS AND STAIRS *70*

17. CROSSES *74*

18. DUALITY *78*

19. CULTURAL REFERENCES *81*

20. SITUATIONS AND SYMBOLS *87*

21. GOING NATIVE *88*

22. SEX, LOVE, AND ROMANCE *92*

23. WEAPONS, WOUNDS, AND DEATHS *97*

24. EXERCISES *101*

CONCLUSION *104*

INDEX *105*

BIBLIOGRAPHY *112*

ABOUT THE AUTHOR *114*

ACKNOWLEDGMENTS

For inspiration: My Texas grandfather, "Daddy Joe" Smith, for my first lesson in symbols — brands on cattle. Illustrator Arthur Rackham's evocative art in Oscar Wilde's exquisite book of *Fairy Tales*. My best school friend, Larry Glazener, with whom I crafted secret code writing in the eighth grade. Manly P. Hall's books and teachings. All my friends and colleagues who work in secret meanings; of course I won't name you.

Thanks to my contributors, readers, and supporters on this book: Monty Hayes McMillan, Georgia Lambert, Aurora Miller, Mike Restaino, Bruce Logan, John Slifko, Ray Boggio, Vanese McNeill, Chance Gardner, Pete McIllwain, Dave Kaplowitz, Kathie Fong Yoneda, Linda Seger, Devorah Cutler-Robinson, Judith Claire, Rachel Ballon, Carolyn Miller, and Ropata Taylor.

Mike Restaino also helped obtain all of the images for this book and deserves a huge thank you for that. And many thanks to the fine publishing team of Michael Wiese Productions.

Special thanks to Bob and Jane Reed, who provided a paradise in which to contemplate deeper meaning.

ïntRoDuctïoπ

Humans are meaning-making creatures. We see animals in the clouds, Mother Teresa on cinnamon buns, and Jesus on rusty screen doors … or was that Willie Nelson?

Communication is the most important aspect of human interaction, and it is accomplished in a number of ways, from utilitarian to artistic. Some of the most primitive yet still most effective modes of communication are visual — that's just how our brains are wired.

About 40,000 years ago humans began creating media. They held their hands against a rock wall and blew out a mixture of spit and pigment, the first airbrushed images. Graffiti tagging begins here.

They dipped tight bundles of hair into hollowed-out stones holding crushed berry juice and with a few exquisite strokes re-created the power and grace of ancient aurocs thundering across open plains. Dapple-rumped deer skittered away from stylized hunters, and fearsome cave bears roared silent warnings to stay away.

How Art Made the World

Sister Wendy: The Complete Collection

Times have changed; the dangers and delights of our world are typically more technological than natural. Yet artists continually brave the impersonal swipes of nature and the devices and desires of the human heart to reveal the truths and mysteries of our existence, to instruct us in its ways, and to revel in its wonders.

In our multicultural, instantaneously interconnected global village, we speak hundreds of languages and thousands of dialects with diverse and specific cultural backgrounds. How can we communicate effectively across all these borders?

Symbols and images affect people emotionally — hence their exceptional effectiveness. Because there is no particular rational attachment to them, visuals are a universal language that engages our intuition and imagination.

Although some of the details may bemuse us, we are still impressed by symbols and images hundreds and thousands of years old. Erotic carvings on temples in India offer enlightenment advice disguised as sexual positions; ancient Egyptian art provides instructions on navigating the afterlife; stained-glass windows and stone carvings in European cathedrals iconize Bible stories for their once-illiterate congregations; and early American builders of massive mound complexes seem to have thought their audience was spirits high in the sky.

People have waged war under symbols: the Roman Empire's eagle (co-opted by the Nazis), the crusader cross of Christendom, the crescent moon of Islam, the hammer and sickle of the Soviet Union. People also accomplish great deeds of generosity and self-sacrifice under icons: peaceful Buddha, Virgin Mary's compassionate sacred heart, the rainbow of many ancient cultures and the modern lesbian-gay-bisexual-transgender LGBT movement. Codes hold and pass on precious or dangerous secrets: Masonic-alchemical-Kabalistic keys to transformation, secret Celtic finger language, Depression-era hobo codes on homes hospitable or hostile, pirates' and spies' maps and markers.

Symbols and images also convey emotions, states of mind, and actions frozen in time. Bernini's exquisite marble statue of Saint Teresa of Avila quivers with the ecstasy of adoration. A flower crushed in bloody battlefield mud captures war's tragic futility.

Kingdom of Heaven

A raised fist commemorates a revolution, a raised flag a victory, and a bird in flight a valiant act or a release to freedom.

The more consciously you use symbols, images, and codes in your stories, the more effective your message will be. Using appropriate visuals will heighten the emotional impact of your story and will connect your audience to the rich stream of meaning — conscious and unconscious — that flows through humanity and our arts.

This book will show you ways that visuals have been used to great effectiveness and ways to do that in your own projects so they too will have more powerful, long-lasting impact.

HOW TO USE THIS BOOK

Keep this book beside your computer as you write your screenplay, novel, or ad copy, and turn to it when you're thinking, "Right, 'Show, don't tell,' but how do I show this emotion?" or "I want something spectacularly visual right here, but what would be the most effective?" or "Everyone in the audience should simply weep now; hmmm … what cue can I give them?" Designed to offer you a panoply of visuals to express and imply emotions, situations, and concepts, this book can help you find a specific if you have the general idea. It can also help if you're already seeing generic visuals in your head but aren't sure how to use them effectively. The Index section helps you cross-reference the specific image to and from the emotion, situation, or concept.

Of course you can do so, but you needn't read this book all the way through to make good use of it. You can approach it like a dictionary or a thesaurus and just pick it up and use it when you want to make an effective visual statement and need some extra inspiration and information.

Here are the sections in each chapter and how to use them.

WHAT IT MEANS

Explanations from antiquity to modern times and across different cultures. Knowing its meaning is essential to using a symbol effectively.

IN HISTORY, MYTH, AND CONTEMPORARY TIMES

Examples sometimes from 40,000 years ago, sometimes from a thousand years ago, sometimes from yesterday's news. That images have been used across the years and cultures indicates their power to convey meaning and can give you ideas on how to use them in your media.

IN MEDIA

Symbols, codes, and imagery occur in all media, and presumably all sorts of media makers will use this book. For the examples, however, I use films, because they are the most universally known and the most accessible. Examples are from the film classics, last year's Oscar winner, cult favorites, or that blockbuster you want to see just one more time. Use these examples as both illustration and inspiration. You can freshen up an old thing by approaching it from a different angle, using a different perspective. Put your unique spin on a symbol and take our breath away with the power of these visuals to bring forth deep emotional responses.

USE

When to use the particular image. For instance, you might want to indicate a particular emotional/psychological state (fear, joy, envy, feeling trapped, etc.); a certain situation (impending danger, camaraderie, rising tensions, etc.); or a concept (freedom, loyalty, spirituality, etc.)

These three levels — emotional, situational, conceptual — expand outward from the most individual to the most abstract.

Use emotional symbols when your character shifts attitude or motive, when you want to signal his or her growth, a failure, a new hope, and so on. An emotional symbol is always very personal and internal and may not necessarily reach beyond that individual. In *American Beauty*, the image of the virginal cheerleader surrounded by rose petals indicated Kevin Spacey's state of mind and emotions. No one else saw that vision.

Use situational symbols when things are changing in the environment or in a group of people. People swept up together in the emotions of the moment often rally around symbols that are political, religious, sports-oriented, cultural, racial, etc. Shifts in economic or social status are indicated via this category of images. In *Gone with the Wind*, Scarlet O'Hara's wardrobe and the condition of Tara symbolized what was going on economically before, during, and after the war.

Use conceptual imagery to indicate higher spiritual yearnings or abstract concepts that are hard to show through action. Trust, loyalty, and freedom are concepts that of course lead to actions, but they start way up in those abstract planes of thought and have a wide-ranging influence on people. Flags, religious icons, and stylized representations typically indicate concepts. Watch Leni Riefenstahl's film *Triumph of the Will* for a superb use of symbols to elicit sign-on to a mythic national cause … or the *Lord of the Rings* trilogy for racial/species warfare causes.

WRITTEN DESCRIPTIONS

In prose you are the director, art director, costumer, makeup artist, and acting coach for every aspect of the story. Sure, you leave some things for the readers' imagination or your story won't engage their imagination, but we want you to create and evoke a rich world for us to explore.

For scripts to be sold and turned into a visual medium, you must first impress a development exec or reader with words on a page. Make your pages incredibly more powerful using potent, visceral words that create vivid images.

Scripts also tell the director, production designer, cinematographer, lighting director, costumer, and actors what you envision. Yes, they'll interpret your vision, but give them solid indications to start with.

Check your thesaurus: for each word listed, you'll find at least a handful more.

CINEMATIC TECHNIQUES

Symbols, images, and codes are only effective when they are appropriately presented, framed, focused upon, and noticed (or not) by your characters. This section presents suggestions on framing, position, lighting, sound, music, and so on, to create the effect you're after.

OTHER EXAMPLES

For further research, and to add your own examples.

INDEX

This separate section at the back of the book will help you find various ways of visually expressing an emotion, situation, or concept by looking it up and then exploring the chapters that refer to it.

HOW SYMBOLS, IMAGES, & CODES WORK

Our brains are built to process shapes. PET scans and MRIs reveal where particular images cause reactions: squares here, circles there, triangles over here.

Some of this is just our animal heritage taken to a more sophisticated level. Baby chicks instinctively run and hide from the shadow of a cardboard hawk. As soon as they hatch, baby ducks imprint as "Mom" the first thing they see. Humans are said to have a "love map" based on their earliest experiences of relationships. Our brains are built to recognize danger as well as positive factors such as good breeding material, healthy food, and safe shelter.

From symbol-recognition survival mechanisms to the subtlety of stylized halos around Stone Age figures (supposedly hallucinations of altered-state artists) to the composition of a shot in a movie to show emotional repression, artists use these tendencies of consciousness to convey meaning and emotion. Unlike talent — which either you have or you don't — the use of symbols, images, and codes is a craft you can develop to improve the effectiveness of your creative projects and to enhance your natural talents.

This language of visual communication has a number of forms and aspects.

✦ Allegory — symbolic representation, often a play on words or actions. *Aesop's Fables* is human psychology illustrated by animal actions: crafty fox, loyal dog, mindless sheep. Fascists and Nazis are evil sorcerers and orcs in *The Lord of the Rings*. Jesus is the lion in *The Chronicles of Narnia*. Other allegorical tales include *Alice in Wonderland, El Topo, The Matrix,* and *The Golden Compass*.

✦ Color — Though color has a universal physiological effect on the eyes, colors have different cultural meanings. In China, white is the color of mourning; in European cultures, it's black. Purple, because the dye used to be so rare, symbolized royalty, the only class who could afford it. Women in red dresses are universally sexy, and scientific studies prove it. Studies also show that blue walls in a room heighten creativity, while red walls heighten memory and lessen creativity.

Lawrence of Arabia

+ Composition — Dynamic lines of tension and isolation of an object, be it still or moving, move the viewer's eye around a frame. One item small and far from a larger foreground item implies a yawning gulf of difference or separation. Move it away from or toward the foreground for significance, like Shane riding away across the prairie at the end of that film (separation and sadness) or Sherif Ali riding across the desert toward Lawrence in *Lawrence of Arabia* (new best friends forever).

+ Exaggeration — Most art is an exaggeration of size, effect, emotion, duration, etc. Hindu sculptures of gods and goddesses emphasize voluptuousness and devotion to the beloved. Picasso, Duchamp, Kandinsky, and other breakthrough artists of early 20th century Europe incorporated mystical philosophies and modern physics into their paintings, exaggeratedly portraying multiple time lines and simultaneous angles of perception.

+ Metaphor — "All the world's a stage", as Shakespeare wrote. Or as Persian poet Omar Khayyam observed much earlier:

'Tis all a Chequer-board of Nights and Days
Where Destiny with Men for Pieces plays:
Hither and thither moves, and mates, and slays,
And one by one back in the Closet lays.

Because we perceive the world through our physical senses, the most solid metaphors are those that reflect physical reality. "Top dog"

"Les Demoiselles D'Avignon" by Pablo Picasso from
Sister Wendy: The Complete Collection

The beloved sled Rosebud — *Citizen Kane*

has a basis in behavior, as does "climb the corporate ladder" or "beat him down." When searching for a symbol for your own visual media, you'll want to come as close to the actual experience as you can and then back off a notch or two for poetic effect.

The spiritual metaphors of ritual — Masonic rites, the Christian Eucharist, many cultures' festivals of light — reflect higher and more abstract concepts.

✦ Synecdoche — the part for the whole. The White House is the U.S. executive branch, Google is an Internet search. In music and visuals it's a leitmotif: a phrase or image that represents a

certain character, situation, or emotion. Think of the "dum-dum, dum-dum-dum-dum" of *Jaws* to announce the shark, or the color red in *The Sixth Sense* to indicate a dead person. In *Citizen Kane* the sled and snow globe are leitmotifs/synecdoches for Kane's childhood.

All of these communication tools can be used in your creative works to speak to the deeper part of ourselves, the meaning-making mechanism that lies within us all. Use them to convey your concepts, to entertain, to stimulate thought processes, to enlighten, and to enrich your audience's experience.

ASTRONOMY & ASTROLOGY

WHAT IT MEANS

Astronomy is the science of stars, planets, comets, and the cosmos. Astrology is a nonscientific system of personality analysis and event prediction based on the movements of heavenly bodies.

IN HISTORY, MYTH, AND CONTEMPORARY TIMES

Since humans first noted the repeated appearance of certain star clusters in the night sky and projected patterns on them, we've had constellations: Leo the Lion, Aries the Ram, Ursa Major, Orion the Hunter. We have also personalized the planets: warrior Mars, lover Venus, speedy Mercury, jolly Jupiter, and gloomy Saturn.

Mayan astronomy was complex and astonishingly correct. Their feathered serpent teacher-god Quetzalcoatl is associated with Venus.

Theories are gaining ground that the Egyptian Sphinx and some pyramids were built to the vernal equinox in the sign of Leo 12,500 years ago.

Athens lost a decisive battle in the Peloponnesian Wars because of belief in astrology.

The Labors of Hercules take him through the zodiac.

The Persian savior god Mithras is shown slaying a bull: interpreted as the precession of the equinoxes as the bull (Taurus) is slain by a warrior (Aries), with many other symbols of the zodiac around them.

King Arthur and the 12 Knights of the Round Table are associated with the zodiac, as are Jesus and the 12 apostles. A pilgrimage to certain Gothic cathedrals retraces the configuration of Virgo, the Blessed Virgin Mary in the stars. Some people claim descent from Sirius or the Pleiades; a stroll down Hollywood Boulevard may convince you that's a possibility.

IN MEDIA

There are a number of films about the real-life Zodiac Killer. Characters in the 1980s typically made lots of references to their astrological signs.

USE

+ To describe a character via their astrological sign: Pisces is sensitive, Leo is egotistical yet generous, Scorpio dangerously sexy, and so on.

+ In the case of astrology, to show a character as woo-woo gullible or, conversely, as sensitive and wise.

+ In the case of astronomy, to imply intelligence, geekiness, an adventurous spirit, an inquisitive mind reaching off planet into the stars. Jody Foster in Contact came to astronomy as a child.

+ In sci-fi and fantasy, the stars are often the very setting of the story.

+ In an aliens-among-us story, it could be the homeland they yearn for or the source of the threat, and you can signal those emotions by showing distant lights in the darkness.

WRITTEN DESCRIPTIONS

In prose, describe the constellation shape. Give your character astrological accessories: a Sagittarius mug, for example, or an Aquarius T-shirt.

For scripts, move the camera across a collection of astrology items. Cut to the night sky. Have characters use a telescope or visit a planetarium.

CINEMATIC TECHNIQUES

Technical enhancement: Draw the constellation pattern; make those stars sparkle more brightly; bring the stars down to earth and overlay them on some other object or surface; turn them into what they represent — a bull, a centaur, a virgin. Reflect the star pattern in a character's eyes, in a pool of water, a glass of wine, a mirror, a window.

Move away from or onto a spinning globe, an orrery, a star chart.

OTHER EXAMPLES

See a planetarium show for clever ways to link viewers' imaginations to the stars.

The Great Work

Galaxy Quest

COMPOSITION

WHAT IT MEANS

The way we put things together tells us much about the importance of one thing to another, the nature of the relationship between them, the history and the future of that relationship. Composition can create tension or relieve it. It can evoke harmony or discord.

IN MYTH, HISTORY, AND CONTEMPORARY TIMES

Art history often categorizes eras and styles based on changes in composition and emphasis. Some Egyptian dynasties are categorized by changes in the color blue. Chinese artistic composition is typically based on even numbers, Japanese on odd numbers.

A major aspect of composition is perspective.

The Hogarth Curve (an "S" curve) is an aesthetic layout found in nature and used by artists to guide the flow of vision around a piece of art.

Feng Shui is the Chinese practice of composing the environment to enhance the flow of energy.

IN MEDIA

The *Da Vinci Code* and *Angels and Demons* books and movies make plot points of the composition of paintings and statues.

In *The Conformist*, directed by Bernardo Bertolucci, the mother, her beauty fading, and her son, ever more distant from her, walk through dead and fallen leaves; the composition says the relationship is decaying.

Bertolucci also places the protagonist of his marvelous film in a swirl, pressed in upon by his wife and his mistress, trapped by other dancers.

USE

+ To indicate a shift in power.

+ To show isolation or loneliness.

+ To emphasize nature over man, or vice versa.

+ To illustrate the scope of a problem.

Triumph of the Will

The Conformist

The Conformist

+ To signal the psychological quality of a character: Show your character against water for an emotional feel, against the earth for a more grounded feel, with the sky behind them for an open-minded feel.

+ In an argument, place the characters so that there's a different and significant background for each, such as a window behind one, a solid wall behind the other; or a wall of books behind one (logical, intellectual) and curtains behind the other (more flighty and insubstantial).

WRITTEN DESCRIPTIONS

Use active, descriptive words: The wall loomed over her, the sea churned behind him, they huddled together, he paced at the foot of the bridge.

CINEMATIC TECHNIQUES

Split screens: The TV series *24* uses multiple screens to give more information and raise the tension. The film *(500) Days of Summer* has side-by-side screens labeled "Expectation" and "Reality," showing what the protagonist wants to experience at a party given by his former girlfriend (them together) and what's really going on (her with her new boyfriend).

OTHER EXAMPLES

Bernardo Bertolucci is a genius with composition. Watch his films *The Conformist* and *The Last Emperor* for exquisite examples of speaking volumes about emotions, situations, and concepts through setting.

3

ΠUMBERS

WHAT IT MEANS

From the infant inspecting her own fingers and toes to scientists running supercomputer equations, numbers have always fascinated us. Some call mathematics the language of the divine, and divine qualities have often been assigned to numbers. Anything that exists can be described in numbers, and numbers often stand in for the thing itself.

IN HISTORY, MYTH, AND CONTEMPORARY TIMES

The earliest writings seem to have been accounting records; those who know numbers — bankers, census takers, and the like — can manipulate those who don't.

The Fibonacci numbers underlie nature's perfect shape, the spiral, and perfect proportion, the golden mean. In this pattern, each new number is the sum of the previous two: 1, 2, 3, 5, 8, 13, 21, 34, and so on. This pattern appears in pineapples, unfurling ferns, seashells, spiral galaxies, and many other phenomena.

Sounds and colors can be expressed in numbers representing their wavelengths. The musical note "A" is 440 cycles per second; the wavelength for the color blue is about 440 nanometers.

Magical Egypt

WHAT THE NUMBERS MEAN

0 — Emptiness, extinction, the void, no thing/nothing.

1 — Unity, wholeness, individuality, isolation, totality, uniqueness, loneliness.

2 — Union, polarity, duality (male-female), balance, connection, entanglement, mating.

3 — Trinity: Many mythologies have a creative trio, often a family structure.

+ Hindu — Brahma, Vishnu, Shiva: creator, preserver, destroyer.

+ Egyptian — Osiris, Isis, Horus: creative spark (father), creative material (mother), creative result (child).

+ Christian — God the Father, Jesus the son, Holy Ghost the assistant. Judeo-Christianity has tried for millennia to keep the feminine out of the equation, but humans inherently go there — hence the persistence of the Virgin Mary.

+ Spirit, matter, consciousness/soul is the trinity of the Mystery Schools.

+ Energy, force, substance — the creative trinity of metaphysics.

+ The eternal triangle of forbidden love.

+ The sexual *ménage a trois*.

4 — Seasons, cardinal directions (north, east, south, west), elements (earth, air, fire, water).

5 — The four directions plus the center pivot pole, tree, arrow, rod, column, etc.

+ Humanity: two arms, two legs, head.

+ Humanity: five senses.

+ Elements in Oriental systems (earth, air, fire, water, metal).

+ Points on a symbolic star. Sides to a pentagram. Percentage of the universe that is visible matter.

Vitruvian man by Leonardo Da Vinci - *The Science of the Secret*

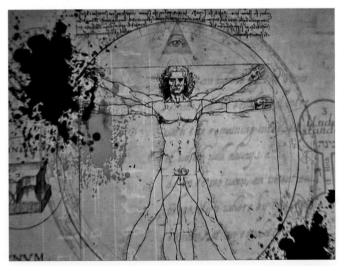

6 — Two trinities, balance, stasis, the connections between spiritual and earthly triads.

7 — The divine trinity plus the earthly quaternary, traditional number of major chakras.

8 — An auspicious number in Burmese culture, influencing even the oppressive military rulers.

9 — The trinity times three, a lucky number for the Chinese.

10 — Fingers and toes, Biblical Old Testament commandments, Sephirot of the Kabala, last days of Ramadan considered especially holy, basis of many mathematical systems.

12 — Solar months, constellations of the zodiac, Labors of Hercules, apostles of Jesus, Knights of King Arthur's Round Table.

13 — Lunar months, the above 12s plus the leader (Jesus plus apostles, Arthur plus knights).

22 — Bones in the human skull, connections in the Kabalistic tree.

23 — Percentage of the universe that is dark matter, arbitrarily assigned significance in Robert Anton Wilson's writings and Joel Schumacher's movie *The Number 23*.

33 — Vertebrae in the human spinal column, steps of Scottish Rite Freemasonry, age of Jesus at his death-resurrection-ascension, Kabalistic connections (22) plus the Sephirot (10) plus the hidden Sephirah, Daath.

40 — Years the Israelites wandered in the Sinai after escaping from Egypt, days Jesus spent in the wilderness being tempted by Satan, days of Lent, Saturn-Jupiter convergences before repeating in the zodiac, weeks of human pregnancy.

42 — The answer to Life, the Universe, and Everything according to Douglas Adams' *Hitchhiker's Guide to the Galaxy*. The number of cell division cycles during human in-utero development.

52 — Number of years in the Aztec Big Sheaf of years.

72 — Degrees in one-fifth of a circle (72 x 5 = 360), number of lawyers at Egyptian bad god Set's trial for killing his brother Osiris, number of virgins allotted a Muslim martyr (an unfortunate mistranslation of astronomical plotting of the heavens), percentage of the universe that is dark energy.

432 — Base number for Hindu Vedic time counts of the cycles of the cosmos.

IN MEDIA

2012 is based on the Mayan calendar's count of astronomical cycles.

In *Se7en*, serial killer Kevin Spacey used the seven deadly sins to plot and execute his murders.

The Number 23 with Jim Carrey.

In *21*, Kevin Spacey is a professor who teaches math whizzes to count cards in Vegas.

USE

+ To illustrate the mysterious complexity of nature. To imply intelligent design. To imply intelligence in a character. To imply madness in an obsessed or OCD character. To signal secret connections to scientific secrets like alien life, weapons designs, new materials.

WRITTEN DESCRIPTIONS

For visual emphasis, use numerical figures rather than words, especially for 10 and above: 22, not twenty-two.

CINEMATIC TECHNIQUES

Have a character write out the number, or if low enough, count it off on her fingers. Have someone count aloud, or physically touch the items being counted. Flash-edit on the things being counted and emphasize it with sound.

OTHER EXAMPLES

A Beautiful Mind, The Da Vinci Code, Angels and Demons, The Lost Symbol.

A Beautiful Mind

4

CODES

WHAT IT MEANS

Superhero decoder rings, secret languages, cryptography ... secrecy and exclusivity are consistent human traits, and one of the best places to hide something is right out in plain sight. Language is a code for meaning, and written language is a code for both sound and meaning. Unlike stand-alone symbols and numbers, a code is a complex system using substitution (this for that) as a guise and requiring a hidden key to unlock.

IN MYTH, HISTORY, AND CONTEMPORARY TIMES

Early tribal codes of smoke signals and jungle drums evolved into Morse code and semaphores.

In Greek myth, Oedipus was the first to successfully solve the riddle of the Sphinx — good thing, because the penalty for failure was death. European fairy tales are replete with riddles involving symbolic codes and wordplays, and the heroes in many stories must solve complex puzzles to win the day.

Braille is a physical code for the blind.

Celtic bards used a secret finger language, touching specific knuckles and joints for specific words; Frank Herbert uses something similar in the *Dune* novels.

The periodic table of elements can be an entire secret code: 8 = oxygen; 6 = carbon, the base of life as we know it; 238 = uranium, used to generate nuclear weapons or power.

Libraries use the Dewey Decimal Systems, websites use URLs, and software is a code.

Cryptography uses codes to transmit hidden messages, be it treasures of the gods, enemy tactics, or assignations for forbidden love. Codes often use keys such as "every third letter in every fourth word" to spell out secrets. Solving Nazi Germany's Enigma code helped the Allies win World War II. Also in WWII, Navajo code talkers simply used their own unique and unfamiliar Amerindian language to foil the enemy.

Encryption is the third step in code-making: 1) Start with letters. 2) Turn them into numbers. 3) Turn them back into different letters — or use symbols and numbers or letters and symbols. Just remember you need two sets of information cross-referenced.

The Mummy

National Treasure

IN MEDIA

Sherlock Holmes excelled at cracking codes. Chess holds the secret code in *The Eight* novel. The Zodiac Killer used astrological signs as a code.

Brendan Fraser and Rachel Weisz break the code in the Book of the Living and release the curse of *The Mummy*.

The paralyzed real-life hero of *The Diving Bell and the Butterfly* employs a code using only his left eyelid to blink out an entire book.

The Da Vinci Code popularized a long-standing premise about Jesus' bloodline.

The *National Treasure* movies revolve around solving codes, and *The Pirates of the Caribbean* trilogy involves verbal riddles and coded maps.

USE

+ To prolong the revelation of and search for specific information.

+ To imply behind-the-scenes machinations.

+ To signal hidden connections to scientific secrets like alien life, weapons designs, new materials.

WRITTEN DESCRIPTIONS

When revealing the code, be explicit: A = 2, B = 3, C = 4, etc.

In the case of an image, be sure you write out the connection; for example, "Her left hand points to the window, but her eyes gaze at the floor", or "He saw the pattern in the bricks and knew it was the same as the pattern of letters to punch on the keyboard".

Make it complex: If a code is easy to understand, it's useless.

CINEMATIC TECHNIQUES

Have a character write out the code correspondences or draw out the design. Use a mechanical device as in *The Da Vinci Code*.

Move the camera between the things you want to connect, or cut directly between them, but have the shots occur in a short period of time.

Multiscreens as in *24* can also be a decoding device: Pull a small insert out to a larger frame size to reveal what was hidden; use multiple layers to unfold a secret; lay a diagram over something, like the pattern of a constellation over the starry sky. In *Duplicity*, multiscreens signal the beginning of a flashback.

OTHER EXAMPLES

Enigma, Windtalkers, The Name of the Rose, Foucault's Pendulum, Frank Herbert's *Dune* novels.

The Da Vinci Code

5

EARTH

WHAT IT MEANS

The physical realm. Nature, stability, solidity; grounded, basic, stolid, unmoving. Creation: Humans are made from clay or earth in many mythologies. The underworld. Death: "Ashes to ashes, dust to dust". Lower status: Rulers and upper classes typically build higher, in the clouds. Fertility, farming, nature's bounty. Source of mineral wealth: oil, metals, gems.

Rocks — stability, solidity, trustworthiness, stubbornness.

Mountains — closer to the spiritual world, challenges to progress, safe havens, holders of high-minded wisdom and secrets.

Deserts — bleak, hopelessness, death. Or sometimes sere beauty. Purity.

Swamps — fetid darkness, hidden dangers, rot.

Plains — blankness, boredom. Or infinite possibility, endless horizons.

Caves — isolation, introspection, spiritual education.

IN HISTORY, MYTH, AND CONTEMPORARY TIMES

Gnomes are the spirits of the earth in Greco-Roman mythology. Norse myths are replete with gnomes and dwarves, dwellers in the deep earth, mountains, and caves.

Beneath Chartres Cathedral in France is the Grotto of the Black Virgin, an ancient site of earth mother worship.

After the flood of Greek mythology, the gods told survivors Deucalion and Pyrrha to toss the bones of their mother behind them. Their mother being the earth, they tossed stones behind them, and from them sprang up a new race of humans.

Earth is typically our mother and the sky our father. In Maori mythology, they lived in a tight embrace for eons until a number of their children, tired of being squashed between them, rebelled and separated the two. Earth goddesses include Gaia, Rhea, Cybele, and Ceridwen.

Land is wealth in most societies, though in many older cultures the idea of anyone actually owning land is laughable. Land rushes and housing booms are modern versions of this affinity for earth.

Some forms of initiation have rites that include earth, with initiates sometimes just handling it as the source of their physical existence, and sometimes being temporarily buried in it as a metaphor for death and resurrection.

Stones are holy in many systems. Stonehenge in England is thought to be both an astronomical device and a religious mechanism. The Kaaba in Mecca, around which Muslim pilgrims walk during the Hajj, holds the Black Stone, a meteorite said to have been given to Ishmael by the Archangel Gabriel. Some interpretations of Arthurian legend have the stone from which young Arthur pulls the sword signify the foundation of life and instinctive wisdom; the sword is then discrimination of mind and intellectual wisdom.

IN MEDIA

The *Lord of the Rings* trilogy gives earthbound beings a hero in the dwarf Gimli. One of the most haunting settings is the Mines of Moria beneath the Misty Mountains.

Mountains and lots of mud stand in the way of building an opera house in the Peruvian jungle in *Fitzcarraldo*.

After the American Civil War, *Gone with the Wind*'s spoiled belle Scarlet O'Hara returns to Tara and personally takes up farming. She grabs a fistful of rich red earth and declares, "I'll never be hungry again".

Deepa Mehta's film *Earth* chronicles a Muslim child and a Hindu child whose friendship is tested when India is split in the late 1940s and violent migrations cause followers of both religions to exchange the very ground they live on.

The desert figures as a character in *Lawrence of Arabia*, grandly when Sherif Ali lopes across the vast stretch of open sand, changing from tiny dot to impressive desert prince; and terrifyingly when shifting sands swallow up one of Lawrence's servant boys.

Gone with the Wind

Lawrence of Arabia

In *The English Patient*, the doomed lovers Count Amalfi and Catherine are buried intimately together during a sandstorm, ensuring the path of their passion.

There Will Be Blood is all about man's relationship to the riches of the earth.

USE

+ To indicate a person's stability, or lack thereof.

+ To widen the effect of the story either by showing how the environment impinges on a character or how a character alters the environment.

+ To give a sense of tradition.

+ To imbue the idea of timeless antiquity.

WRITTEN DESCRIPTIONS

Use your thesaurus for earthy terms: loamy, dusty, clay, marl.

State what the earth means to a character: a trap, fertility, security, a challenge.

Give the earth a voice: Rocks speak, mountains sing (as, one might say, in *The Sound of Music*?), dunes or prairies hum, pebbles on a beach growl.

CINEMATIC TECHNIQUES

Shoot from "on the deck", close to the ground.

Use mud or dust on your characters and sets to indicate despair, or engagement with basic survival, or discovery of riches.

In an exchange of dialogue or argument, put the earth behind the more logical person and perhaps water or fire behind the more emotional person.

Rate people or situations using the symbolism of metals, graded from coarseness to fineness, or rarity to commonness: iron, copper, silver, gold, platinum — and that Hollywood favorite, "unobtainium."

Use a tripod or plate and keep the camera steady — no nausea-cam.

Focus on some aspect of earth as your earthy character begins to speak, then move to the character.

OTHER EXAMPLES

The Treasure of the Sierra Madre; Grapes of Wrath; King Solomon's Mines; Bad Day at Black Rock; The Mummy; Journey to the Center of the Earth, preferably the 1979 version; *A River Runs Through It; The Thin Red Line,* Terence Malick's gorgeous paean to earth; *Days of Heaven; Giant;* the opening of *Predator,* where the alien hunter parachutes down to earth; *300,* with the mountain pass; and *Cool Hand Luke,* with Paul Newman digging away on the prison chain gang.

6

AİR

WHAT IT MEANS

Freedom. The very essence of life itself: You can live without food for weeks, without water for a few days, but without air for only a few minutes.

Spirit. Since you can't see it but you can see its powerful effects, air is often given godly status. Wind is the messenger of the gods: The random breeze can bring illumination; the flight of birds spurs inspiration; the fury of a storm is divine punishment.

Superhuman power. Unlike building dams to hold water, putting water on fire, or molding earth to our plans, we humans find controlling the air really difficult.

Understanding. We call vague ideas "cloudy," we bemoan the "fog" of war, we strive for mental "clarity." In this sense, air is directly connected through vision to insight.

IN HISTORY, MYTH, AND CONTEMPORARY TIMES

Creation myths often begin when a divinity exhales the very cosmos, or breathes life into inanimate objects, transforming them into living, breathing creatures.

Thunder gods and storm gods abound, most of them powerful and fearsome.

Prana is the essence of life in many Oriental systems, and its main carrier is the air, the breath. Most yoga and meditation systems involve control of the breath.

Air spirits are sylphs in Greco-Roman mythology.

"The Birth of Venus" by Sandro Boticelli — *Sister Wendy: The Complete Collection*

Pegasus the winged horse (symbol of the Ajna chakra) is a higher manifestation of the centaur (symbol of the Sacral chakra); the wings indicate freedom from ties to the earth, freedom to roam the world.

Legend has it that real-life court adviser and reputed magician John Dee helped save Elizabeth I's England by conjuring up wind-whipped storms that wrecked the Spanish Armada.

Some winds are so upsetting to humans they not only have names — sirocco, simoom — but some cultures also waive crimes committed when these hot, dry winds howl in off the desert. So far Los Angeles has not implemented a "Santa Ana wind" defense, but give us time.

Some prophecies about the early 21st century predict killer wind-storms, rather like those hitting Europe too often these days.

IN MEDIA

In *The Iliad*, King Agamemnon sacrifices his daughter Iphigenia to bring winds to move the becalmed Greek fleet off shore and on to Troy. He pays dearly for that upon his return 10 years later when his Queen Clytemnestra, still upset about the sacrifice of their daughter, stabs him to death.

In *Dead Calm*, a lack of wind brings terror for sailing couple Nicole Kidman and Sam Neill.

Dead Calm

In *Master and Commander*, the ship at full sail is a glorious vision of air in motion, taking the valiant men off on an adventure.

Judi Dench is an air elemental in *The Chronicles of Riddick*.

Zephyr is the Greek west wind, a demon boss in the game *Castlevania: Dawn of Sorrow*, and a character in the *Golden Sun* game.

Master and Commander: The Far Side of the World

The Kite Runner

USE

+ When a character desires or obtains freedom: Jonathan Price as the angelic birdman in *Brazil*, escaping his oppressive office cubicle to fly above the dark city.

+ To show a radical change from one state of being to another, as in the leap of faith, a birth, or a death.

+ To indicate aspiration and hope, typically with something rising on the wind: a bird, kite, balloon, leaf.

+ To signal a touch of suspense, magic, or mysticism via a flickering candle, the curtain blowing in a random breeze, a lock of hair lifting, a door slamming shut.

+ No movement can signal statis or boredom; peace and calm typically occur in a story before or after turmoil.

+ Storms and frenzy indicate turmoil. Many horror films use storms to signal unrest, dangerous powers on the loose.

+ Swift movement signals progress, hope.

WRITTEN DESCRIPTIONS

Use descriptors for air straight from the weather channel: gusty, calm, cloudy, clear, crisp, swirling, brisk. Dare to be poetic: serene, crystalline, shoving, nudging, swirling, and so on.

Indicate what reacts to the movement of air: a dress, a scarf, trees, clouds.

CINEMATIC TECHNIQUES

Since air is invisible (unless you count smog), you need to show some other thing being affected — or not — by it: leaves fluttering in the breeze, trees bowing in a gale, clouds rushing across the sky, a character leaning into the wind.

Include flying creatures and objects (birds, butterflies, balloons, kites, planes) to illustrate the state of the air, and thus either a situation or the temperament of higher powers: political, familial, social, divine.

Show trees bent over in the wind as a metaphor for a character who yields but does not break.

OTHER EXAMPLES

The Perfect Storm, Twister, The English Patient.

7

FIRE

WHAT IT MEANS

Destruction. Purification. Transformation. Divinity. Passion. Anger. Ambition. Hell.

IN HISTORY, MYTH, AND CONTEMPORARY TIMES

Greek Titan Prometheus defied the old gods' system to bring fire to lowly mortals but was severely punished for his generosity.

Salamanders are a fire symbol, as are dragons in many systems. In Chinese rug iconography salamanders mean long life.

When Norse god Odin had to put his favorite daughter, the warrior princess Brunhilde, to sleep on a rock as punishment for disobeying the law, he placed a protective ring of fire around her so only a valiant knight could reach her, wake her with a kiss, and claim her as his own. The Hindu god Shiva dances in a ring of fire.

Many myths and the symbols thereof show hearts on fire; a line from *The English Patient* says that the heart is an organ of fire; Elvis admitted being a "hunka hunka burnin' love," while Johnny Cash and June Carter sing of love's "ring of fire". Anyone who's ever been madly in love, passion, or lust knows well those fiery qualities.

Hindu god Shiva dancing in a ring of fire - *The Great Work*

Cremation of dead bodies is a tradition in many systems and is typically thought to help release the soul from the physical form. Vikings placed their dead warriors fully armed on a boat, often with their favorite dog, then set the boat on fire and pushed it out to sea.

The Professional

IN MEDIA

In *Patriot Games*, Sean Bean dies on board a small boat in flames, but the camera cuts to a close-up of his face just before the explosion. This is interesting in that he is a bad guy but is given the respect of a great warrior as in a Viking funeral.

In *The Professional* Jean Reno surprises the guy who just shot him by handing over a grenade pin from the explosive vest he's wearing. They both end in fire.

Fire, by Deepa Mehta, explores the dangerous passions of both traditional and rebellious love in an Indian family.

Ralph Fiennes' Count Amalfi is ruined by fire in *The English Patient*.

The fire strike at the end of *Apocalypse Now* destroys Colonel Kurtz' compound and suggests the cleansing of that evil aberration of power and violence. Not coincidentally, the film starts with a fire bombing of the jungle.

Willem Dafoe's Raven walks through fire in the 1984 rock'n'roll classic *Streets of Fire* to challenge Michael Pare's Tom Cody. Both men have a fiery passion for singer Ellen Aim, played by Diane Lane, and will fight it out on the streets.

This walking through the fire is echoed in the first *Terminator* film, where it really seems that this creature came straight from hell.

Fire in *Crash* brings transformation of racial and class prejudices when Matt Dillon's Ryan rescues Thandie Newton's Christine from the fire in the SUV.

Streets of Fire

Crash

USE

+ To indicate passions out of control.

+ To signify transmutation from one state of being to another.

+ To warn of danger.

+ To condemn to hell.

+ To tantalize us with the promise of passion.

WRITTEN DESCRIPTIONS

Use associated words such as kindling, spark, flame, fume, smolder, blaze, smoke, cinder, ashes, singe.

In a script, because of production logistics, consider how close you need a fire to be to people or things. Any kind of real fire is both expensive and dangerous. Can you get the symbolic effect by shooting through or close on a small contained flame? Or can you use special visual effects and still get the story impact you want?

CINEMATIC TECHNIQUES

You're lucky here because fire, unlike air, is actually visible.

Framing a character against fire illuminates the character's primal threat.

Flickers of flame can indicate a potential problem that, unless contained, can blaze up into a holocaust.

Cutting between a romantic or sexual scene to flames of any sort carries the message of passion.

Sometimes just shooting through heat waves will give enough indication of fire, and that can be done with a heater in front of and below the lens.

OTHER EXAMPLES

Die Hard II has the bad guys crash and burn at the end. In *Independence Day*, the alien blasts cause fires all around the planet. *Lost in Space. Backdraft. Batman Begins.*

8

WATER

WHAT IT MEANS

Emotions, emotions, emotions.

Fecundity. Growth. Refreshment. Sexuality. Birth. Hidden depths. Death by drowning.

The source of all life. The formlessness to which the form returns after death.

The mysterious. Lost civilizations. Hidden cities. Forbidden knowledge.

Rain can be sorrowful, joyful, dangerous. Snow can be peaceful or smothering. Storms on land or sea are typically symbolic of tempestuous emotions. Steam can symbolize contained emotions, heated up to the boiling point, in danger of burning the unwary.

IN HISTORY, MYTH, AND CONTEMPORARY TIMES

Though many creation stories have us made from clay, others see the sea as our origin. Sea foam is likened to semen in many myths, inseminating the feminine earth. Aphrodite, the Greek goddess of love, arises from sea foam, most famously portrayed in Botticelli's portrait of her on a half-shell.

Ondines are the water spirits of Greco-Roman mythology. When Jason and the Argonauts — Hercules among them — go in search of the Golden Fleece, Hercules' boyfriend Hylas is seduced to his death by these water nymphs, breaking Hercules' heart and diverting him from the quest.

Pisces the Fish is considered the most emotional and sensitive astrological sign.

Mystic Christianity notes that Moses parted the Red Sea, symbolizing the old way of walking through the emotions, while Jesus calmed the stormy sea and walked upon the water, symbolizing the new way of rising above the emotions and holding rational thought.

Many "foundation" myths include a great flood that destroys a great civilization or a great number of people. Atlantis and Lemuria have the grandest mythic scope, and paleogeology does chart out a number of actual floods that could have been the source of such racial-memory-become-myth instances. Floods and tsunamis have plagued humans as long as we've been humans; today's technology affords us more knowledge about them all.

An iceberg brought down the *Titanic* and gave us the most dramatic shipwreck of modern times. Icebergs are now melting across the globe, and the polar ice sheets are thinning dangerously.

IN MEDIA

Considered near scandalous in 1953, the beach kiss in *From Here to Eternity* has the lovers drenched in water, pounded repeatedly by the relentless waves of … you get the idea.

Shakespeare's *Tempest* begins with a storm and goes on with interwoven story lines of emotions such as revenge, greed, and passion.

D.H. Lawrence writes in *Women in Love* of a young couple drowning in a lake immediately after their wedding, leaving no doubt that he sees marriage as a deadly emotional trap.

The crucified Jesuit missionary going over the South American falls at the opening of *The Mission* nicely signifies that colonial attempts to control the natives may not be working. The emotional strength of the indigenous people might be temporarily swayed by Catholicism, but like the forest, hills, and rivers, their traditions are very old and very strong.

In *The Year of Living Dangerously,* Mel Gibson's character admires a beautiful young woman who dives into a

leaf-covered swimming pool at a rundown resort. He later dreams that he dives into the murky water to save her, but she tries to drown him. This perhaps symbolizes the unused and rotten resources and emotions of the people, politics, and situation in 1967 Indonesia: Beneath the natural beauty is corruption and impending death.

From Here to Eternity

The Year of Living Dangerously

Script consultant Linda Seger points out the use of water imagery in *The English Patient* to signal sensuality and emotional connectedness.

Mary Shelley's novel *Frankenstein* begins and ends in the frozen Arctic wastes.

That exceedingly popular movie about young love on the high seas, *Titanic*, wouldn't have been nearly as effective had Jack not drowned, leaving Rose and her newly awakened emotions clinging soggily to her memories, and millions of young girls sobbing at the poignant beauty of lost love.

Sailing ships play a big part in many adventure stories, some of the best being Patrick O'Brian's *Master and Commander* series, where the valiant men work both with and against the majestic seas.

And let us not forget surfing films: *Big Wednesday, Endless Summer, Point Break, Blue Crush,* and, okay, *Surf Nazis Must Die* (yes, I've seen them all).

USE

+ To indicate various emotional states. Frozen water equals frozen emotions. Lack of water equals lack of emotions. Gushing water equals contained emotions finally freed. Steam equals dangerously repressed emotions.

+ To emphasize a shift in emotions, a character's inner transformation.

+ To punctuate a shift in situations, typically something that affects lots of people and the environment — negatively or positively.

WRITTEN DESCRIPTIONS

Use adjectives and verb forms that apply to both water and emotions: flowing, frigid, moist, damp, and so forth.

In a script, communicate the quantity so filmmakers can create the effect you intend: looming ice cliffs, trickling stream, rising tide, soaked with sweat.

CINEMATIC TECHNIQUES

You have a wide array of approaches with water since you can focus on a single tear quivering on an eyelash or show a tsunami sweeping over a mountain range.

Wavy lines are the symbolic shorthand for water, as in much primitive or stylistic art, or the astrological sign for Aquarius.

You can also use fish to draw attention to water. Tropical fish in an aquarium, a print or statue of a dolphin, a whale fin necklace.

The opening of *The English Patient*, with swimmers floating in paint across paper and then seen frozen on sandy desert cliffs, is an excellent example of using liquid to evoke emotions and plot points without using water itself.

An emotional turning point in *Blue Crush* is appropriately set in a lagoon, with the surfer girl and her boyfriend, both fully dressed, arguing about her fears and how to get over them. Following his encouragement, she goes on to surf Pipeline.

Isolation and contrast are major factors in symbolism, so set your "small-water moment" against a contrasting background: a single drop of water in the dust, a rivulet of sweat on an otherwise dry body, one glass of icy water in a steamy setting.

A major emotion associated with water is the fear that we'll be overwhelmed. To give your audience that sense of impending discomfort or doom in a "large-water moment," set the lens below the midline of the water so we're looking up at it. Or have the frame filled two-thirds or more with the water/ice/storm/steam, either vertically, horizontally, or diagonally.

Blue Crush

OTHER EXAMPLES

Martin Sheen rising from the river in *Apocalypse Now* is so iconic it's copied over and over. *Waterworld*, *Castaway*, *Run Silent Run Deep*, Deepa Mehta's *Water*, *The Hunt for Red October*, *The Abyss*. Ice and snow are featured in a number of movies: the 1998 *X-Fil*es movie, *Ice Runner*, *The Ice Storm*, *The Thing*, *The Day After Tomorrow*, and the TV reality series *Ice Road Truckers*.

9

AΠiMALS

WHAT IT MEANS

The outstanding characteristic of a given animal: crafty fox, coura-geous lion, wily serpent, silly goose, loyal dog, independent cat.

Its environment or situation: alpha male, free as a bird, extinct as a dodo, pathetic as a caged chicken, fantastic as a dragon, mystical as a unicorn.

A concept: Birds often represent the soul (personal incarnation) or spirit (eternal life force). The egg is a universal symbol of genera-tion, possibility, new beginnings. Helen of Troy and her siblings Clytemnestra and Castor and Pollux are often shown popping out of eggs laid by their mother Leda after her rape by Zeus in the form of a swan.

IN HISTORY, MYTH, AND CONTEMPORARY TIMES

From *Aesop's Fables* to *The Chronicles of Narnia*, from the dog-headed Egyptian god Anubis to Scooby Do, we've always used animals to symbolize aspects of human nature.

Pantheons are rich with animal gods, part-animal gods, and mixed-animal gods. Angels have bird wings. The Babylonian teacher god

Oannes was fish on top, man on bottom — or maybe just a smart sailor wearing chain-mail armor.

Tribes and clans have totem animals, and nations have symbolic animals. The Roman Empire, Nazi Germany, and the United States all chose the eagle.

The Science of Secret

Bats are used in Chinese rugs to symbolize happiness. In Western lore they often symbolize vampirism.

From weretigers to centaurs, humans are often shown as part animal to symbolize an internal or external meaning. Esoterically, the centaur is the Sacral Center/chakra, meaning the animal nature (lower half) still controls where and how the human nature (upper half) goes.

Astrology uses animals to signal the main psychological aspect of many signs: Aries the Ram, Taurus the Bull, Pisces the Fish, and so on.

In many mythologies, the concept of nature's interconnectedness is symbolized by the spider.

Animals are often combined: The merlion of Singapore melds a lion head and chest, representing the city-state's prowess on land, with the lower body of a fish, symbolizing its marine riches.

How Art Made the World

IN MEDIA

Individuals have spirit animals. Many shamanic tribes use animals as archetypes and messengers. The shamans and sometimes ordinary people in altered states access these totems. In *The Emerald Forest*, Westerners experience the indigenous tribes' magical relationship with animal spirits.

In *The Golden Compass*, characters have their own animal daemon always beside them. It is the creature of their persona: Daniel Craig's snow leopard, Nicole Kidman's golden monkey, Sam Elliott's hare.

Anthropomorphized animal characters have been around probably since humans began. You can find plenty of them in cartoons, fantasy stories, and games. Sometimes they run true to the stereotype, but sometimes not at all.

USE

+ To elicit a strong, immediate identification of some specific emotion, situation, or concept.

The Golden Compass

+ When you need to go in-depth about a character, quickly.

+ To create allegories about human individuals, types, or situations. George Orwell's *Animal Farm* is a great example.

WRITTEN DESCRIPTIONS

Use pets, jewelry, collections, memorabilia, settings (parks, zoos, the jungle, the veldt) to connect an animal and its attributes with a character. The girl who collects unicorns is vastly different from the guy who collects dragons. Use animal terms: She stalked in, cat-like; he swooped down on them; the sergeant roared; she slithered through the crowd.

CINEMATIC TECHNIQUES

Include the animal in the same frame as your character. Or cut/pan/ tilt from the animal to the character either before or after, depending on the effect you want. If it's before, you put the audience in the know; after, you either inform them about what they just saw or affirm their perceptions. It's more subtle, but you can also move the camera as the POV of the animal: swooping birdlike from on high, crouching close to the ground, leaping catlike from spot to spot.

OTHER EXAMPLES

The Chronicles of Narnia, Beowulf, The Jungle Book, Anne McCaffrey's *Dragonriders* stories.

10

CHAKRAS

WHAT IT MEANS

An awareness of human psychology and physiology, as well as esoteric knowledge. Certain specific ways of feeling and acting according to which Center of Motivation (chakra) your character is focused in right then.

IN HISTORY, MYTH, AND CONTEMPORARY TIMES

This ancient system of character analysis shows up in most cultures' myths, from Greek Odysseus' travels home from Troy, to Pueblo Indian sand paintings, Tibetan tankas, and Mesopotamian sculptures.

Christian iconography shows Saint George stabbing the dragon in the Throat (intellect) and Saint Michael stabbing the dragon in the Heart (emotions).

New Age followers use the chakras for self-analysis and self-improvement.

Most Easterners have been familiar with them for millennia, and more Westerners are familiar with chakras today, so you will be able to use this system of symbolism with more freedom than before.

Sumerian tree of life, the Louvre – photo by the author

Certainly you can use it subliminally, but because of this growing awareness, you can also be outright and direct in referring to them. Like any good symbol system, the chakras carry lots of psychological and spiritual weight.

WHAT THE CHAKRAS ARE

Physiological bundles of nerves along your spinal column that connect to various organs that create hormones and affect your emotions. There is a wealth of information about the chakras available in books, classes, websites, and films. My own book *INNER DRIVES*, also by this publisher, is one.

The chakras, what they signify, and some film examples:

+ Root — sheer survival, death / *Dark Knight*'s Joker.

+ Sacral — sex, fear, money / Nicole Kidman in *Moulin Rouge*.

+ Lower Solar Plexus — individuality, exclusivity, power, me-me-me / all the actors in *Tropic Thunder, Rocky*.

+ Aspirational Solar Plexus — inclusivity, generosity, altruism, spirituality / Harvey Milk in *Milk*, Dev Patel in *Slumdog Millionaire*.

+ Heart — self-sacrifice for the greater good / *Joan of Arc, Gandhi*.

+ Throat — communication, art, finance, statecraft / Spock and Data of *Star Trek*.

+ Ajna — integrated, balanced collaboration of all other chakras, control central / Frodo in *The Lord of the Rings*, Neo in *The Matrix*.

+ Crown — connection to a higher spiritual self, greater awareness / angels, gods in myriad films.

IN MEDIA

In *Jacob's Ladder*, Danny Aielo is a chiropractor who plays the psycho pomp (guide to the other world) to Tim Robbins' fatally wounded Vietnam vet. Chiropractic medicine works with the chakras, and Aielo helps Robbins move his consciousness up from the Root chakra to the Crown chakra (see *INNER DRIVES*, p. 218).

Groundhog Day also follows a character up through the chakras as he learns not to be a self-centered jerk but to consider others, fully engage, and thoughtfully consider his creative actions (see *INNER DRIVES*, p. 215).

In *The Matrix*, Neo wakes up naked with wires plugged into his chakras, feeding him the sensation of being in a "real" world. The chakra at the base of his skull is called "The Mouthpiece of God."

In *The Lord of the Rings*, Minas Tirith has seven levels with a gate between each one and a tree at the summit. There's also a tower and a "seeing eye" similar to the third eye (Ajna) atop the staff (spinal column) in many cultures' iconography of the chakras.

Jacob's Ladder

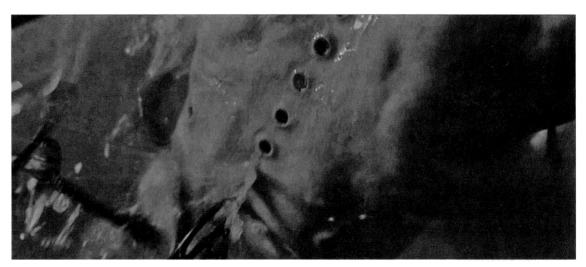

The Matrix

USE

+ To add a metaphysical aspect.

+ To indicate a person's cultural background in Oriental or ancient mystical philosophies.

+ To label someone as New Agey, either positively or negatively.

+ To tie in ancient traditions with modern practices.

+ To tap into an archetype and connect it to your character.

WRITTEN DESCRIPTIONS

Use a few words to explain the chakras. For instance, if a character refers to the Solar Plexus, have another character ask about it so you get in a bit of explanation for your reader, assuming that your audience is not already knowledgeable about chakras.

If you want to be more subtle, just indicate the body spot of the chakra you want to emphasize — for example, "He balls his fist tightly into his waist" for the Solar Plexus; "Her hand wandered to her throat, playing with her necklace" for the Throat chakra; "The old man rubbed his forehead thoughtfully" for the Ajna.

In scripts you can write in those specific actions as directions.

CINEMATIC TECHNIQUES

Use the symbol for a chakra in the background, as an icon in the props, or as part of a character's wardrobe, for example, a centaur for Sacral, a bull for Throat, fire for Sacral, and so on.

Select a color palette consistent with a particular chakra.

All this information is available in greater detail in *INNER DRIVES*.

OTHER EXAMPLES

In my book *INNER DRIVES: Create Characters Using the Eight Classic Centers of Motivation* (chakras).

COLOR

WHAT IT MEANS

Humans only perceive a small portion of the light in the universe. Our visible spectrum is limited to the rainbow of colors but does not include ultraviolet, infrared, and the myriad of other wavelengths. Different wavelengths affect our brains in different ways, a fact that is no doubt the basis for the ritual and subliminal use of color by most cultures throughout time.

The day-night quality of our earthly existence may be the reason we often assign goodness (sunshine, visibility, comfort) to white and evil (darkness, secrecy, danger) to black. Vampires reverse this, and sci-fi stories speculate how a two-sun system or other arrangement might affect psychology, sociology, and religion.

Colors describe emotions: She's blue, he's green with envy, they saw red, a black mood, purple with rage.

Whether by psychological affinity or astonishingly strong coincidence, colors have taken on character:

+ Pastels are soft and innocent.

+ Jewel tones are strong and have integrity.

+ Yellow hues are stimulating, blue hues soothing.

+ Red excites; in studies, women wearing red are deemed the most sexually attractive.

+ Mourning colors vary with culture, time, and fashion.

IN MYTH, HISTORY, AND CONTEMPORARY TIMES

Based on their artwork, earlier humans and some current cultures seem to perceive only primary colors … or have a visual affinity for gold.

Age takes away from our abilities to perceive the full spectrum of colors, as evidenced by those elderly women whose garishly bright makeup looks just fine to them.

Our industrial and fashion color palettes shift every few years and give identity to a period: avocado and earth tones for the 1960s, Mediterranean pastels for the mid-1980s. However, ancient Egyptian art was static for centuries, then saw an explosion of a new blue that itself lasted for centuries.

The chakras are assigned different colors in different systems.

Many initiatory systems use colors to denote steps along the path, such as white belt to black belt in the martial arts.

Religious rituals assign different colors to different seasons and occasions.

When Greek nature goddess Demeter's daughter Persephone was kidnapped by Hades, the world lost its color as the mother mourned her loss. Color returned to the world when Persephone returned, thus explaining the changing of the seasons.

A good reason for red uniforms? They don't show blood that might upset the soldiers.

THE COLORS

White
All colors combined and reflected, the unseparated spectrum. Purity. Innocence. Goodness. Emptiness, formlessness, inescapable sameness. Death pallor, bloodlessness, a blinding void and cause for deep instinctual panic. Moby Dick is all the scarier for being pure white. In American Westerns, good guys wear white hats and bad guys wear black. People at leisure or in positions of power often wear light colors to say, "I'm in no danger of getting dirty."

Black
All colors combined and absorbed. The unknown. Mysterious. Sophistication. Secrecy. Evil. Death. Darth Vader would not be nearly as effective in pale blue. *Women in Love* is set in England's coal mining country; the miners are covered in black, denoting ignorance and poverty, while the heroines are smart, intelligent girls decked out in rich colors.

Blue
Innocence, connections, correct relationships, loyalty (true blue), cool, freedom, exploration, clarity, emotional. Gods and goddesses often wear blue and sometimes *are* blue. The blue-skinned Na'vi in *Avatar* reflect the Hindu source of the word "avatar."

Red
Blood, sex, danger, strength, vitality, heat, anger, purpose, power, stimulation, urgency. In *The Sixth Sense*, red indicates the presence of the spirit world.

Yellow
Sunlight, warmth, awareness, lassitude, bright intelligence, cowardice.

Green
Life, nature, growth, nurturing, soothing.

Purple
Deep, reflective, contemplative, royal, priestly, divine.

Orange
Argumentative, combative, crisp, sharp, mental, alert.

Gray
Somber, sober, grim, lifeless, doomed, sophisticated, shy. *Pleasantville* uses grays and color to contrast conservative small-town attitudes with sexual awakening and lively joy.

The Sixth Sense

Pleasantville

Brown

Earthy, solid, sturdy, luxuriant, grounded, dependable.

Metallics

Preciousness, weaponry, technology, impermeable, strength, rigidity.

Gold

Riches, quality, warmth, solar.

Silver

Coolness, remoteness, lunar.

Each color varies from light to dark, faint to saturated, and you can select a shade along the scale that is appropriate for your character or situation. Also, you can find myriad charts for color interpretation of many other hues.

IN MEDIA

Both *Schindler's List* and *The Sixth Sense* use red against a grimmer or a cooler background to emphasize the personal impact or the uniqueness of the situation.

In *Schindler's List*, the little girl in the red coat is one person going against the tide of the horror occurring around her, just as Schindler would soon go against the tide of Nazi oppression as he helped save Jews.

USE

+ To signal specific moods for your characters.

+ To elicit certain reactions from your audience.

+ To emphasize a shift in emotions or situation. In *The Sixth Sense*, red means "Undead nearby ... beware!"

+ To highlight something.

+ To show contrast between characters and/or situations.

WRITTEN DESCRIPTIONS

Include emotionally descriptive words: grim gray, bouncy yellow, shy teal, monkish brown. Link colors with other senses: piercing yellow, screaming orange, silky gray.

CINEMATIC TECHNIQUES

The same color appears different according to its surroundings (see Joseph Albers' book *Interaction of Color*), so do visual tests before final printing or filming.

Select your basic palette (two or three main colors) and include accents for visual emphasis. Assign characters their own main color.

Use color to show your characters' transformation throughout a story: Start with very pale and increase the intensity of the hue as characters get stronger, or the reverse if they are losing power.

Schindler's List

As characters become closer, bring their colors closer in hue: He wore blue, she wore green; as the relationship develops, each adds more of the other color. Think of tourist couples who dress alike.

Use color as rebellion. The kid from the conservative family puts on bright orange, neon green, and silver.

OTHER EXAMPLES

The English Patient uses the contrast of sere yellows for the dangers of the wartime desert and watery blues for the sensuous emotions. *The Red Shoes* are vibrant symbols of a dancer's passion for her profession as well as the love triangle that dooms her.

12

THE LEAP

WHAT IT MEANS

The best stories are about transformation — sometimes external, sometimes internal, usually both. A character transforms, a situation transforms, the environment transforms. The exaggerated transformations in stories give us examples of how to approach the changes in our own lives.

Showing characters actually leaping from one physical spot to another symbolizes a shift into a different state of being. Initiatory systems often use the Leap to symbolize a change from childhood to adulthood, single to married, outsider to insider.

Dramatic conflict surrounds this pivot point in a story, because once characters make such a radical shift, the old ways no longer work, and it often takes them a while to adjust to the new way. They can yearn all they want for the old way, but there's just no going back.

Philosophically, this image of the Leap says a lot about the unstoppable passage of time and how it affects us all.

IN MYTH, HISTORY, AND CONTEMPORARY TIMES

The Tarot card of the Fool symbolizes the initiate starting out on the journey of discovery, the Hero's Journey. He is poised to step out into thin air and looks pretty happy about it. For many others, it is not a welcome step but rather a move of desperation. Like it or not, when you step off the edge, some sort of transformation is guaranteed.

IN MEDIA

The Fugitive Richard Kimble (Harrison Ford), wrongfully accused of murdering his wife and determined to find the one-armed man who actually killed her, must stay out of jail to do so. Eluding the law, he makes a desperate leap out over a dam and into a swift-flowing river. Now presumed dead, Dr. Kimble is able to pursue the search for the real killer. The Leap typically symbolizes the death of the former self and a new beginning.

Pursued by a posse with no chance of escaping back the way they came, Butch (Paul Newman) suggests to Sundance (Robert Redford) that they take a leap into the river below at a pivotal moment in *Butch Cassidy and the Sundance Kid*. When Sundance

The Fugitive

Butch Cassidy and the Sundance Kid

protests that he can't swim, Butch blithely replies that given the height and the swiftness of the river, it'll hardly matter. They jump. Though the tone feels light, this is life or death for our antiheroes. Butch and Sundance escape this time and do try to go straight. But it doesn't work out, and they eventually meet death in a rain of lawmen's and soldiers' bullets. Here the heroes were not able to leave their former lives behind.

Sometimes the Leap is done not for the self but for others, often at great cost. In the instance of *Indiana Jones and the Last Crusade*, the motivation is love. Indy's father is dying, and only Indy (Harrison Ford) can save him by finding the Holy Grail somewhere across that deep chasm. This is truly a Leap of Faith, as the bridge is invisible until he steps onto it. Change is often like that — impossible to imagine until you actually do it.

Occasionally the Leap is literally from one state of physical existence to another. What begins as a run from unsatisfying lives goes horribly wrong in *Thelma and Louise*. Thelma (Geena Davis) and Louise (Susan Sarandon) have killed a rapist and are surrounded by cops. Deciding they can't turn back but will bravely go together for total transformation, the two grasp hands and hurtle out over the edge of the canyon into another state of being entirely.

Killing off your heroes can be dramatically affecting. Just be certain you've justified it throughout the story and have given enough of a setup that it doesn't feel false.

USE

+ To shift the pace or tone of the story, as at act breaks.

+ When your characters or a situation has reached a seeming Point of No Return. To show that what's behind is undesirable and what's ahead is unknown. There should be some obvious risk and some personal sacrifice involved. Sometimes the sacrifice is of a way of life, or social connections, or a treasured object. Sometimes it's life itself.

+ The Leap is not effective if there's a sure thing on the other side, so work in ambiguity. Make the leaper unsure of the reward, or unsure if there even is a reward for taking the Leap.

WRITTEN DESCRIPTIONS

Exaggerate the contrast between one location and the other, play up the disparities: vast chasm, gaping distance, dizzying height, yawning gulf.

State specifically what the two locations offer: independence vs. oppression, freedom vs. prison, life vs. death.

CINEMATIC TECHNIQUES

The Leap is usually best viewed from a number of angles. You'll want a wide establishing shot to give the sense of how dangerous this is. There needs to be an over-the-shoulder from the leaper's POV to place us within her feelings. We also want to look up at

Indiana Jones and the Last Crusade

Thelma and Louise

the leaper and see the facial expression: is he confident, terrified, resigned? Then, depending on your budget, there should be at least one side shot of the Leap itself, in addition to the wide shot, plus follow-on coverage of the other angles during the Leap.

Depending on the situation, this is typically best accomplished with a multicamera setup rather than a repetition of the often dangerous and complicated live-action part of a Leap.

OTHER EXAMPLES

In *The Wild Bunch,* the antihero outlaws leap their horses off a high railroad bridge into a river and head down into Mexico to exile and extinction. At the end of *Crouching Tiger, Hidden Dragon,* the warrior Jen leaps off the bridge to "return to the desert" and her beloved. *Lethal Weapon, Temple of Doom, The Great Escape,* and *Starship Troopers* all have significant Leaps.

13

ANATOMY

WHAT IT MEANS

The function of that body part: life force (blood), new life (sex organs), perception (eyes, ears), speech (mouth), motion (legs), connections (hands), identity, consciousness, ideas (head).

Psychiatrist Sigmund Freud famously observed, "Anatomy is destiny": Our bodies greatly determine our experience in and with the world. Just as gods supposedly make humans in their own image, humans fashion our creations in our own image, including our gods.

Just as faces the world over look the same when experiencing the same emotions (that's why cartoons and emoticons work), media makers also use body parts to convey emotions, situations, and concepts.

IN HISTORY, MYTH, AND CONTEMPORARY TIMES

Egyptian temples often reflect human anatomy, from the brain to the full body.

Native American kivas used for community and spiritual events reflect the womb, with entrances through birth canal-like tunnels or navel-like openings.

Hindu statuary reflects the dichotomy of gender with the stone lingam (penis) and yoni (vagina).

Christian cathedral entrances, with two towers and arched doorways topped with round windows, resemble a reclining woman with her knees up — accepting the seed of devotion, giving birth to religious blessings. Saints are often shown surrounded by the pointed oval of the Vessica Piscus, which resembles female genitalia.

Magical Egypt

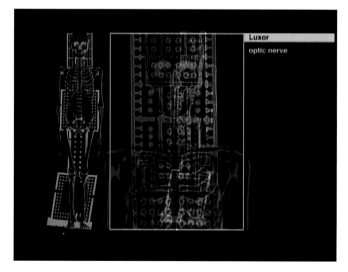

Mixed species such as Egyptian animal-headed gods, Greek centaurs, Sumerian winged lions, and Incan jaguar priests convey special powers. Mixed species like the robotic Cylons and the Borg are unsettling, often terrifying. The elephant-headed Hindu god Ganesha symbolizes good-natured persistence rising above adversity.

Werewolves, weretigers, and other human shape-shifters emphasize an animal characteristic actually manifesting in the body of the human. That's much more inconvenient than just wearing animal skins or a bear-head helmet, but it's also much more powerful for your stories.

Distortions or disfigurement seize our attention. Some say it's an impersonal, instinctual reaction to a defect that may weaken or harm the herd. At the extreme of that, zombies definitely catch our attention.

Both giants and tiny people convey emotional states, such as arrogance or powerlessness, and situational states, like oppression or cleverness, operating below the level of common awareness.

Many people note the resemblance to the human fetus of images of supposed extraterrestrial aliens.

WHAT THEY STAND FOR

Head — consciousness, intelligence.

Skull and Crossbones — the pirate flag and the symbol for poison. For some secret societies this refers to the two seats of creativity

The Great Work

— brain and loins. Both skulls and eggs are symbols of fertility, imagination, and physicality.

Pineal gland — Buddha's topknot, the pomegranate, the pine cone, and the pineapple in spiritual iconography all physically resemble the pineal gland, the gland of the Crown chakra.

Eyes— perception, special abilities, psychic vision, wisdom. "You are being watched."

A university study reports that when pictures with eyes in them were put up in a coffee room, the people acted more honestly.

Ears — perception, cognition, awareness.

Hands — ability to make and do things. Relationship to others: closed equals shy, snobbish; open equals generous, friendly; fist equals scared, angry.

Mouths — communication, sexuality.

Heart — compassion, love, sacrifice, courage.

Blood — life force, compassion, familial connections.

Arms — strength, protection, ability to carry.

Legs — mobility, strength, ability to support, sexuality.

Sex Organs — stereotypical characteristics: male equals outgoing, aggressive, bold; female equals receptive, nurturing, collaborative. Regeneration.

Tunnels, chutes, ducts — Whether it's the birth canal (seed in, baby out) or the alimentary canal (food in, waste out), tube shapes imply transformation, a transition from one state of being or awareness to another. Hopi myths tell of migrating through tunnels to new worlds.

IN MEDIA

Beauty and the Beast stories speak to both our lower and higher natures, as well as warning us to look beyond appearances. See variations on the Beauty and the Beast concept of odd anatomy in films such as *Elephant Man*, *The Man Without A Face*, and Jean Cocteau's 1946 *Beauty and the Beast*.

Villendorf Venus - *How Art Made the World*

Modern advertising often uses the headless bodies or otherwise isolated body parts of women (and sometimes men) to promote things often having little direct relation to the body. But as the saying goes, "Sex sells."

The Playboy Bunny sequence in *Apocalypse Now* makes extravagant use of anatomical symbols with the breast-shaped lights and the phallus-shaped missiles decorating the concert set.

Cult favorite *Boondock Saints* uses a tunnel sequence to birth the twin vigilante boys from behind the scenes to up-front and very noticeable to both the mob and the FBI.

Apocalypse Now

One of the scariest monsters ever is H.R. Giger's anatomically distorted creature in the *Alien* series, while the shambling creature-humanoid aliens of *District 9* and the lizard-humanoids of *Alien Nation* engender more sympathy than fear.

USE

+ To show the audience something your characters may not be aware of.

+ To convey a backstory or connection that would take too long in exposition.

+ To add emphasis to subtext.

+ To externalize a character's emotional wounds or weaknesses.

+ To create unease or sympathy in your audience via the distortion of human anatomy.

WRITTEN DESCRIPTIONS

Use direct reference. Use secondary reference via "like" and "as" to create connections between a body part and another item: "The walls embraced them like welcoming arms."

When referencing a specific body part, use one of the descriptive words from the lists above to signal your intent: "strong legs," "sad eyes," "broken heart."

In a script, point out anatomical references to your reader/director/ art director so they know to focus on that during filming: "The eyes of the portrait seem to follow them across the room."

CINEMATIC TECHNIQUES

Highlight the actual body part with lighting, focus, or against a vague or disparate background.

Place an image of the body part (marble head, painting of hands, etc.) in the set, and depending on the story point you are making, either let it be subtle such that the audience notes it but the characters do not, or have a character note it directly by looking at it, touching it, or making a comment about it.

Reveal the similarity to or disparity between normal anatomy: Show the mechanical insides of the cyborg. This biomechanical aesthetic was most effectively visualized by H.R. Giger and has been the inspiration for many other aliens and monsters (see *www.hrgiger.com*).

Be aware of the "Uncanny Valley" syndrome: As robots or computer graphics get too close to human appearance, a rejection factor sets in — "That's not right!" If you want to create unsettling images, go there. If not, then make your robots or CGI humanoids obvious creations rather than almost human.

OTHER EXAMPLES

Tunnels: *Galaxy Quest, Mission Impossible, The Last Starfighter, Great Escape, Die Hard.* Phallic imagery: *Dr. Strangelove, Armageddon, The Right Stuff.* Size disparities: *Honey, I Shrunk the Kids; The Incredible Shrinking Woman; The Incredible Shrinking Man; Land of the Giants; Short; Fantastic Journey; My Giant; Iron Giant; Iron Man.* Hybrids: the *Star Trek* Borg, the *Battlestar Galactica* Cylons, the Terminators.

14

CLOTHES

WHAT IT MEANS

Character, status, mood, group affiliation, sexual preference and availability. The outer presentation a person makes to the world. What they want others to think and feel about them. Clothes make the man, woman, child … any character. Why else have an Academy Award for Costume Design?

IN HISTORY, MYTH, AND CONTEMPORARY TIMES

The first fashion show may have been fig leaves and animal skins, but humans quickly discovered that clothes could display rank and enforce our tendency to establish hierarchy. Castes and classes delineated themselves with special outfits. Tribes and families created their own color schemes — such as the famous Scottish clan tartans — or other distinct patterns forbidden to outsiders.

The Shipibo of Peru create designs that reflect geometric patterns of energy, which can also be expressed in song. Those patterns are believed to connect their ancient culture with the spirit world.

Aztec priests wore filthy black bloodstained robes; other ancient priestesses wore all white. Catholics and some Protestant denominations have different-colored raiment for different events and seasons in the church calendar.

Purple was expensive to produce in preindustrial times, so typically only royalty wore it. Some societies regulated who could wear which colors under sumptuary laws to ensure that only the higher classes could look like the higher classes. Basically it was a law against knockoffs.

Clothes can express political positions, religious affiliations, clan ties, and tribal histories. Some societies resist change at all costs, hanging onto styles and costumes even unto death.

Attire can show a person's comprehension or disregard of a society's rules: For example, in the American South you're not "supposed" to wear white before Memorial Day or after Labor Day. Men who wear conservative clothing all week long in the office rebel in parrot-bright togs on the golf course.

Sexual availability or prohibition is often signaled with clothing styles, particularly in more conservative cultures.

IN MEDIA

Dressing up is a favorite pastime for most girls. The construction of Cinderella's ball gown is a fun sequence in that animated movie. The same concept is at work in *Pretty Woman*, where prostitute Julia Roberts goes from the L.A. streetwalker look to Beverly Hills chic.

A running gag in the delightful British TV series *Jeeves and Wooster*, starring Hugh Laurie and Stephen Fry, is the all-knowing butler Jeeves' disapproval of the airheaded aristocrat Wooster's choice of sartorial splendor.

When Marlene Dietrich first wore slacks, it stirred a scandal. Check her out in a Navy uniform in *Seven Sinners*.

USE

+ To show a shift in status, as with Eliza Doolittle in *My Fair Lady* transforming from street to salon, or a shift in profession, as in *Working Girl* when Melanie Griffith goes from secretary to executive.

+ To show a particular state of mind. In *Love Actually*, a young man in love with his best friend's new bride is torn between hiding his feelings and declaring his love. He wears a four-panel suede sweater-jacket and turns back and forth in the street. The distinctly

Pretty Woman

Pretty Woman

separate panels indicate his diverse emotions and, along with the turning, give us a real sensation of his dilemma.

✦ To put someone in disguise: Jack Lemmon and Tony Curtis in *Some Like It Hot*, Dustin Hoffman in *Tootsie*, Jennifer Garner in *Alias*.

WRITTEN DESCRIPTIONS

Use adjectives that describe emotions or attitudes as well as the clothes: button-down banker, straight-laced church lady, punked-out slacker, pink Polo preppie. In prose you can become very specific with descriptions of clothing, and it can really help your reader enter the world of your story and characters.

In screenplays you generally do not want to describe wardrobe in detail unless it is essential to the story or character. Words indicating style will give an idea of what you want but still let the director and costume designer make the creative choices. You could use words like "loosely flowing," "street punk," "lost in another decade," and so on.

Working Girl

Working Girl

Love Actually

CINEMATIC TECHNIQUES

Show the person getting dressed. Show them shopping, as in *Pretty Woman*. Do close-ups on specific items, as in the opening shots of *Patton*.

Have the person's actions point out the item — doffing a hat, putting on or taking off gloves, fidgeting with buttons.

Use a left-behind piece of clothing to show abandonment or death: the usually controlled man inhaling the fragrance from his ex-lover's silk garment and finally breaking down in tears; the parent hugging the dead child's pajamas.

SPECIFIC CLOTHING ITEMS

HEADWEAR

WHAT IT MEANS

Social or political status. State of mind. Religious position.

IN HISTORY, MYTH, AND CONTEMPORARY TIMES

Chieftains wear the most impressive headdresses, generals have the most trim on their caps, and church ladies vie for most elegant Easter bonnet. Princesses wear delicate, sparkling tiaras, whereas queens wear heavy, bejeweled crowns.

The Phrygian cap symbolizes freedom, from the Roman Empire to the American and French revolutions. Esoterically it's sometimes said to represent the male sex organ. What it symbolizes for the Smurfs is anybody's guess.

A beret can top an affected artiste, a revolutionary, or a dangerous Special Forces trooper.

Religions vary on covering the head when dealing with divinity, from shaved bald to full veiling. Some systems bare the head the better to receive the deity's energy; others cover the head so as not to get blasted by the deity's energy. With that same deity-receptor concept in mind, sometimes men bare their heads but women cover theirs, and sometimes vice versa.

Buddha's topknot symbolizes the pineal gland of the Crown Center/ chakra. The Egyptian Ureaus signals the kundalini energies raised up for conscious use of the pituitary gland and the Ajna Center/ chakra. Most priestly headdresses reflect these universal spiritual principles.

IN MEDIA

In the old Westerns, the good guys wore white hats and the bad guys wore black hats.

Women's hats can be exceptionally stylish and flattering but are often trifles, sometimes garish or outright ridiculous. A hat can say a lot about a lady; it can even let you know she's not a lady.

All well-dressed men of modern times wore hats until President John F. Kennedy did not wear one to his inauguration in 1961. It was the death of hats on American men. You can see how sophisticated they looked by watching episodes of the TV series *Mad Men*, film noir, and most media of the first half of the 20th century.

That beat-up dusty old fedora that Indiana Jones wears just really says, "Adventure!" So much so that before we see him in the 2008 *Indiana Jones and the Kingdom of the Crystal Skull*, we first see the fedora.

Baseball caps have been ubiquitous on American guys for the last 30 years, and whether it's turned forward or backward is subject to local fad and interpretation. Mostly it's meant to say, "I'm cool. I belong". Too often it says, "I have no individual sense of style and am a total fashion victim."

USE

+ To show vulnerability (taking off a hat) or determination (putting one on).

+ To show respect by doffing a hat or taking it totally off; or to show lack of respect by keeping it on in inappropriate places. Musician Joe Cocker croons, "You can leave your hat on" during a seduction song; not very typical, that.

+ To change a character's mood.

French sailor in a Phrygian Cap
Master and Commander: The Far Side of the World

Indiana Jones and the Kingdom of the Crystal Skull

MASKS

WHAT IT MEANS

A different identity. Something hidden. Something assumed, rightly or not. Mystery. Crime.

IN HISTORY, MYTH, AND CONTEMPORARY TIMES

Whether a smart-aleck Cro-Magnon teen or a serious shaman first put an animal's head atop his own, rites and ceremonies have included masks that imbue the wearer with the qualities of that representation. The king stag for Celtic fertility rites, bull heads in ancient Crete, and jaguar masks in Mesoamerica all recognize and typically honor the connection between human and animal kingdoms.

Psychologically we are all thought to have many masks, and a great part of the work with a professional is to uncover and develop one's own authenticity.

In esoteric teachings, the personality of this particular lifetime is often referred to as the mask the soul wears while in incarnation. The work of spiritual disciplines is to learn about the distinction between persona ("mask" in Greek) and the soul and how to use the persona as an instrument of the soul.

Most of us play various societal and relationship roles. Annual masked revels are a tried-and-true safety valve against getting too stuck in the role and forgetting who one really is. Many societies celebrate role reversals, with the peasant playing king for a day and the bosses kowtowing to the lowly servants.

Secret societies often don masks and/or hoods, as in the American South's Ku Klux Klan.

IN MEDIA

Well, Jason and that hockey mask. And then there is the classic *Man in the Iron Mask*. *Black Orpheus* is set in Rio de Janeiro during carnival, and the heroine is pursued by a man masked as Death.

Pirates stereotypically have an eye patch, and it's often associated with adventure, derring-do, and a brave, impetuous personality. In *300*, the eye patch marks a deadly warrior. In *Sky Captain and the World of Tomorrow*, Angelina Jolie plays a brave, daring pilot warrior. Commander Franky Cook wears an eye patch and is in perfect control of her ship and her men, to the admiration of old flame Jude Law and the jealous consternation of girl reporter Gwyneth Paltrow.

Masks often cover disfigured faces, as with Darth Vader in *Star Wars* and the manipulative mentor in *Phantom of the Opera*.

Bad guys typically wear masks. A comic touch is achieved in the surf movie *Point Break* when the bank robbers wear masks of former presidents. In a flip of that stereotype, the Lone Ranger, a good guy and law enforcer, wore a mask.

Sky Captain and the World of Tomorrow

Stanley Kubrick's last film, *Eyes Wide Shut*, features a secret society and sex rituals performed by masked initiates, including Tom Cruise.

USE

+ To hide a mystery, as in who killed the duchess at the masquerade ball?

+ Fancy-dress balls are easy ways to reveal the inner lives of your characters, and almost everyone enjoys them.

+ To reveal something inside characters that even they didn't know was there. The anonymity of a mask allows deep and often primitive feelings to emerge.

SHOES

WHAT IT MEANS

Profession. Lifestyle. Mood of the moment. Social status. Sexuality.

IN HISTORY, MYTH, AND CONTEMPORARY TIMES

Cinderella's slipper these days is clear glass; in older versions it is fur-lined. Both are said to symbolize female genitalia.

Chinese foot binding imposed three-inch embroidered silk slippers symbolizing feminine daintiness, dependency, and desirability. Adults had to break the young girls' feet and bind them tight to make them fit the tiny shoes. The women could only hobble about, bound by this imposed concept of beauty and sexual fetishism.

In ancient Egypt men wore high heels to exaggerate their sexuality, and Restoration England and prerevolutionary France saw men in fancy high heels below colored tights and short pants. The genders have switched fashion sides, and now Carrie Bradshaw of *Sex and the City* prances down Fifth Avenue in sky-high Manolo Blahniks under very short skirts.

Twisted Roman emperor Caligula's name means "little boots." When he was a little boy on maneuvers with his soldier father, he demanded his own pair of boots, then pranced around showing them off and becoming the darling of the troops.

IN MEDIA

Flashdance spawned many of the '80s fashions, but most impressive was Jennifer Beals unlacing her steel-toe welder boots and prancing barefoot out onto that dance floor.

Sex and the City: The Movie

Hans Christian Andersen tells the story of the red shoes, in which a vain girl puts her fancy new shoes above even other people and so is cursed to always dance in them. Trying to escape the endlessly dancing shoes, she even cuts off her own feet. In this fairy tale about the dangers of obsession, the girl eventually finds redemption and peace. A 1948 movie about a ballerina tells a parallel story in *The Red Shoes*.

Even the title of the romantic comedy *Barefoot in the Park* uses the symbolism of no shoes for a carefree spirit.

USE

+ To show a change in mood: from carefree (barefoot, sandals, tennis shoes) to responsible (dress pumps, lace-up brogans) or vice versa.

+ To give a sense of sensibility: sophisticated, casual, chic.

+ To signal a particular profession or hobby.

+ To indicate moving on, or escaping.

+ For romantic seduction or sexual activity, as when Carrie and Big reconcile in the *Sex and the City* movie.

UNIFORM

WHAT IT MEANS

Belonging, lack of individuality, devotion to a cause, being trapped by a system, order. For superheroes the uniform is often part of their tool kit.

IN HISTORY, MYTH, AND CONTEMPORARY TIMES

Uniforms are perfect for keeping track of your team and your status. They're also valuable for equalizing a disparate group of people.

It's easy to keep track of rank when everyone is dressed similarly: You just keep adding stripes or pips or ribbons. Or in the case of martial arts, you just change the color of the belt.

Priesthoods typically have uniforms to set them apart from the rest of society. Generally speaking, these uniforms are rather shapeless and are meant to cloak the wearers' humanity. Except for the higher orders and during the performance of rites, the uniforms also tend to be drab, since a strong aspect of the path of religion is turning away from the material world.

The Big Lebowski

IN MEDIA

Of course war films feature uniforms. So do sports films. Typically the opposing sides will be in different uniforms so we can tell who's winning the fight. A point of rising tension is when you cannot tell the sides apart because the uniforms are too similar or there is a coup, or perhaps trickery.

In the classic film *Zulu*, the contrast between warring nations is embodied in the Zulu warriors' climate-appropriate and totem-based uniforms of animal-skin kilts, bare chests, and lion mane headdresses against the British Army's heavy red wool uniforms that cover the entire body. The sweating Brits start looking awfully tattered by the end of the day's long battle, but the Zulu warriors still look sharp. Their salute to the British at the end is all the more poignant for that sense of warrior-to-warrior connection despite the vast chasm between cultures and couture.

Though Norse and Celtic women were noble warriors, for the most part a woman putting on a uniform is still unusual. In most Joan of Arc films, much is made of her donning armor. In *Private Benjamin*, Goldie Hawn's struggle with an Army uniform is part of the comedy.

Robert DeNiro in *The Mission* goes from a conquistador captain to a penitent in priestly garb. Exchanging one uniform for the other is meant to make him change his character from hot-tempered to submissive, but that only works for a while, and by the end of the film he's back in his true warrior mode.

During a hallucination in *The Big Lebowski*, Jeff Bridges' Dude wears an oddball uniform cobbled together from what's been going on in his life, from a bowling tournament to Saddam Hussein and the first Gulf War, to strong sexy women.

A really clever sequence in *The Incredibles* is when Mr. Incredible goes to costume designer Edna "E" Mode for a new uniform and gets that hilarious lecture on why "No capes!"

USE

+ To illustrate a transition into or out of an emotional state of mind.

+ To indicate a character's acceptance or rejection of authority.

+ To see that a character is holding onto order in the midst of chaos.

+ To let us know that a character is clinging to the past by still wearing some part of an old uniform.

+ To show a shift in situation: donning the uniform means war has begun, taking it off means peace.

+ To signal a concept like nationalism, patriotism, bravery.

ARCHITECTURE

WHAT IT MEANS

Usually a situation or a concept rather than a personal emotion or characteristic. The mud hut denotes poverty, the luxurious palace prosperity. The jumbled streets of a slum say something vastly different from the broad lawns of a gated community.

Lofty arches and oversized rooms imply power, creativity, and technical prowess. There is also neurophysiological evidence that high ceilings promote more imaginative thinking.

Bridges connote connections or transitions.

Fences and walls mean barriers, separation, challenges.

High ceilings encourage lofty thoughts; low ceilings are oppressive.

Domes and rotundas are natural acoustic amplifiers and typically connote political or religious power.

Windows: Looking in implies covert observation. Looking out can suggest a desire to be somewhere else, or that the mind has gone elsewhere, imagining, remembering....

Mirrors: reflection, being once removed from a situation, memory, identity, unexpected insight, spying, secrecy.

How Art Made the World

Doors are psychological or situational portals from one thought or emotion or state of being to another.

Tunnels also imply a transition from one state to another, just as the birth canal conducts us into the world.

Towers are typically confinement, often for princesses or wizards.

The Great Work

IN HISTORY, MYTH, AND CONTEMPORARY TIMES

Architecture is specifically designed to "say" something.

Many initiatory systems use doorways as tools to signal the psyche that a change is occurring. You are taught to "become the door" in order to pass through it.

As seen in the Anatomy chapter, some Egyptian temples are exact replicas of the human brain or other parts of the anatomy, and specific rites were conducted in each area to affect specific aspects of the body or consciousness.

The golden mean or ratio of 1-1.618 is a mathematical proportion said to create the most pleasing shapes in nature and has been used for aeons in architecture.

Sacred architecture is often said to replicate the energetic shape of the resident spirit; some psychics "see" the construction of a colorful form during religious services. Minarets, onion domes, cross-shaped cathedrals, and nested enclosures (inner sanctums, holy of holies) are all said to reflect these spiritual forms.

IN MEDIA

The 1927 classic film *Metropolis* is a brilliant example of architecture as social commentary, with oppressed workers trudging on dangerous assembly lines for the enrichment of corporate overlords (sound familiar?). This futuristic story of haves vs. have-nots, revenge, robots, true love, and justice relies heavily on visual meaning. The machine becomes a monster like some bloodthirsty temple god, consuming the workers.

Another futuristic film, the dark, wet *Blade Runner*, has become synonymous with overcrowded, over-commercialized urban living. *The Fifth Element* has a similar architecture but with brighter colors and a wackier story.

Metropolis

Metropolis

In *My Life as a House*, Kevin Kline has a terminal illness; building a house tracks and epitomizes his physical decline simultaneously with his building a soul and growing as a person.

Hogwarts School for Witchcraft and Wizardry has fascinating architecture, from the crenellated towers to the moving staircases, floating light fixtures, and loquacious paintings, all refusing to conform to the laws of muggle physics. Harry Potter's alma mater proudly says, "Different World!"

Walls can show barriers between people.

Bridges are signals of transitions from one way of being to another, or of connections between opposing forces. Richard Wagner's Ring Cycle operas show the gods marching over the Rainbow Bridge to Valhalla, leaving the world below to men. This is echoed in the backstory of *The Lord of the Rings*.

The Bridge on the River Kwai uses the image of the bridge to convey chain-of-command ties between British soldiers and officers, reluctant respect between the Japanese and British commanders, William Holden's identity shift, Alec Guinness' switch back from misguided collaborator to loyal saboteur, and the emotional and ethical chasms reluctantly crossed in any wartime situation. *Tropic Thunder* marvelously spoofs the blowing-up-the-bridge scene.

Mamma Mia!

USE

+ To convey a concept above and beyond the dialogue and action.

+ To signal an inner shift in a character's emotions.

+ To indicate a specific status (rich, poor, strong, shaky) in a situation, person, or group.

+ To show a shift in situation (sturdy to crumbling, secret to open, etc.).

WRITTEN DESCRIPTIONS

Describe your characters' feelings in direct relation to the architecture. Looming architecture dwarfs people. Vast structures isolate them. Cozy ones comfort a character. Lofty shapes can inspire the soul; cramped shapes can imprison it.

CINEMATIC TECHNIQUES

For architecture to matter, you have to make it more than just a set. Linger on it at the beginning of a scene. Show it first without people. Play the camera over the contours of the item: Zoom in and out across a bridge; tilt up from the floor to a high door, arch, tower, or building; move in to a barrier, stop, then cut to the other side. Shift lighting and/or pacing if using different rooms to denote internal change.

In *Elizabeth, the Golden Years*, placing the camera very high and shooting down at her in the bottom of a well of cold stone walls shows her heartbroken, betrayed, and confined by the duties of her crown.

OTHER EXAMPLES

German Expressionism is full of architectural symbolism — always compelling, often disturbing. *Metropolis, The Cabinet of Dr. Caligari, From Morning Until Midnight, Nosferatu,* and most Fritz Lang films. Leni Riefenstahl's *Triumph of the Will* makes powerful use of both interior and exterior architecture.

Tropic Thunder

Elizabeth: The Golden Age

16

STEPS & STAIRS

WHAT IT MEANS

Progress. Ambition. Accomplishment. Struggle. Improvement. Dissolution.

Upwards — spiritual progress or attainment. Death and transfiguration. Ascent into the heavens. Gain of place and status.

Downwards — spiritual decline or condemnation. Death and descent into the underworld. Destruction. Loss of place and status.

IN HISTORY, MYTH, AND CONTEMPORARY TIMES

Maybe it started when we climbed down out of the trees, but humans have always been fascinated by steps and stairs and tend to give them meaning beyond just the utilitarian. Whether it's the stairway to heaven or the steps into the scary dark basement, our meaning-making minds impose transition into the picture.

Most initiatory systems include steps both symbolic and actual. Esotericists point out that mystic Christianity had 33 stairsteps to the Upper Room, Masonry has 33 degrees, Jesus is said to have been 33 years old at his crucifixion and resurrection, the Kabalistic tree has 10 sephirot, 22 paths, and 1 void, for a total of 33. By

no small coincidence there are 33 vertebrae in the human spinal column. Climbing the stairs symbolizes the rise of consciousness, kundalini energy, spiritual awareness.

Since many deities live on high, religious structures typically have steps leading to an altar or central spot of worship. Priests, pastors, and imams usually climb steps up to a lectern or minbar high above the congregation.

William Blake's *Jacob's Ladder* painting is one of the most famous stairs images, bringing to life the Old Testament story of Jacob's dream of a stairway to heaven.

Though we didn't know about it until the mid-20th century, the structure of our DNA is like a spiral staircase, so now you can also be referencing evolution and the mysteries of creation when you show that shape.

IN MEDIA

A classic comic bit is Laurel and Hardy wrestling the piano down the staircase. The tumble down the staircase in *Whatever Happened to Baby Jane?* graphically signals (or IMs) the character's fall from fame to obscurity and madness.

The Cabinet of Dr. Caligari uses stark lighting and askew camera angles to create unease around a staircase.

And of course there's the poster-worthy shot of Rocky running up the steps in Philadelphia, arms raised in victory, the perfect symbol for reaching your personal goal.

Alfred Hitchcock's classic *Vertigo* uses steps and stairs to create suspense, a sense of danger, and breathtaking horror.

In *Jacob's Ladder*, Tim Robbins' dying Vietnam vet, finally accepting his fate and letting go of physical life, sees his deceased young son atop a staircase, bathed in light. Releasing anguish and regret, he rises to meet his beloved boy.

Before getting their slogan-spurring "Mission from God," the *Blues Brothers'* Dan Aykroyd and John Belushi "visit the Penguin," a nun. As they mount the stairs to her office there is intimidating *Cabinet of Dr. Caligari* lighting and angles. As they leave, they tumble down the stairs.

My favorite example of steps and the effectiveness of image referencing is found in a trio of films. First, in the classic *Battleship Potemkin*, a baby carriage bounces down the wide Odessa Steps during the military repression of a popular uprising. Protestors and innocent civilians are being shot down in the panic, including the baby's mother. The sequence symbolizes the brutality of the state

The Battleship Potemkin

versus the rights of the people and how whenever larger powers fight, lesser people suffer.

This powerful imagery was replayed seriously in Brian De Palma's *The Untouchables,* as federal agents Kevin Costner and Andy Garcia play out a botched stakeout on the wide staircase in a train station. The mother and the baby carriage raise the dramatic tension, and the reference to huge power groups battling and innocents suffering is unmistakable.

The Untouchables

In the comedy *Naked Gun 2 1/2*, the Odessa Steps scene is re-created in an over-the-top fashion, with not only a baby to save but also the pope and the president. The bad guys are not just one monolithic oppressor but also include, among others, disgruntled postal workers.

Naked Gun 2 1/2: The Smell of Fear

USE

✦ To indicate a shift in identity or state of being.

✦ Death. Ascent into heaven or the vast beyond. Descent into hell or a vast unknown.

✦ Acquisition of new knowledge or perspective.

WRITTEN DESCRIPTIONS

Both prose and script: Tell us about the pitch of the stairs — steep, shallow, wide, gradual — as it will describe the nature of the revelation.

In a script, if you're referencing another film — as *The Blues Brothers* does *The Cabinet of Dr. Caligari* and *Naked Gun 2 1/2* does *The Battleship Potemkin* — put the reference in there explicitly so your readers and realizers know what to re-create.

CINEMATIC TECHNIQUES

Shoot from both the bottom and the top of the steps to get as much coverage as possible so that when it comes to editing, you can get really creative, even if a character is ascending or descending into another world and we are not going to enter that world.

Also get side shots and if possible the extremes of a) shooting from above the stairs (not on either end but straight down on midflight, with a jib arm) and b) a POV of whoever's going up or down the stairs. If they're tumbling or sliding down the stairs, your dolly grip and crew will have fun with that rigging.

Shoot close-ups on the feet going up or down the steps.

Use variable speeds to effect a disorientation, a floating sensation, reluctance to transition.

To emphasize a transition from freedom to confinement, start wide and narrow the focus as you go up or down; for a transition to a freer state, start narrow and widen out as the character reaches the next flight up or down.

If following a character up or down a spiral or a well staircase, rotate the camera around the vertical axis to increase the sense of internal transition, and to heighten tension.

OTHER EXAMPLES

The Bourne Identity, The Professional, I Robot, Metropolis, Giant, Gone with The Wind, Long Kiss Goodbye, Armageddon, Star Wars Revenge of the Sith, Bananas, Love & Death, Brazil, The French Connection, The Third Man, The Italian Job (both versions), *True Lies.*

17

CROSSES

WHAT IT MEANS

The coming together of two different things, ideas, systems, emotions, perspectives. The binding of two disparate things. Spirit/soul trapped in matter. Suffering, sacrifice, and redemption.

IN HISTORY, MYTH, AND CONTEMPORARY TIMES

The cross is a symbol of sacrifice in many cultures. It is also symbolic of nature's aspects. The four elements and four cardinal points of the poles easily form crosses, as do the seasonal solstices and equinoxes.

Esoteric symbolism sees the cross as a combination of inner and outer. The placement of the crossbar is indicative of the progress of the individual: The higher the crossbar, the higher the consciousness.

The Egyptian ankh is said to symbolize the womb and birth canal. Some also see it as a very stylized head and body with arms outstretched.

The Norse god Baltar was hung on a cross, the Persians' virgin-born god Mithras was crucified, and so were many other gods, including of course the Christians' Jesus.

The cross both terrifies and reassures: It symbolizes both a brutal death and a glorious rebirth into a better life.

Christians of the 12th and 13th centuries carried the cross on Crusades. The symbol for the famed Knights Templar was a red cross.

The Hindu hooked cross symbolizing peace was subverted into the Nazi swastika, which reversed the direction of the hooks as well as the meaning.

Magical Egypt

Kingdom of Heaven

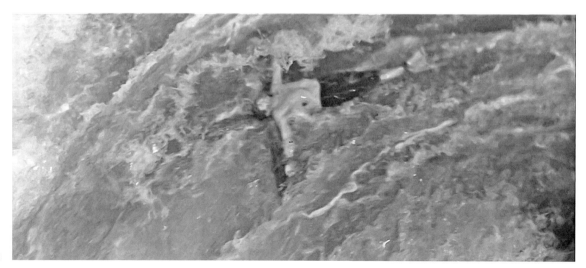

The Mission

Crossroads are considered dangerous places where evil spirits can enter our world. Legend has it that the brilliant bluesman Robert Johnson got his talent when he made a deal with the devil at a crossroads. Eric Clapton sings brilliantly about it in "Crossroads."

The Red Cross and Red Crescent officially merged and morphed into the nonreligious Red Crystal in 2008.

IN MEDIA

In *The Mission*, a crucified Jesuit missionary hurtling over South American falls signifies that the colonialists' attempts to control the natives may not work. It's a visual slap in the face for a religious empire that for 1,400 years had specialized in assimilating local religions. The empire strikes back and that is the core of this story, but the locals and their Catholic missionary accomplices do give a good fight.

All the Jesus films and most Christian-based Biblical stories include the Crucifixion.

Monty Python's *Life of Brian* is a clever take on the life of a chosen one ... sorta chosen, anyway.

USE

+ To signal a meeting of elements traditionally at odds.

+ To indicate sacrifice.

+ To indicate compromise.

+ To indicate Christianity.

+ To ward off vampires, demons, evil.

WRITTEN DESCRIPTIONS

Include the dichotomy of opposites in the symbolism itself: divinity and humanity, conservatism and liberalism, and so on. Someone can be "poised at the crossroads, crucified on their own indecision."

In scripts, be explicit so your readers and filmmakers don't miss the sign: "She holds her arms out as though on a cross."

CINEMATIC TECHNIQUES

Use this symbol as a revelation or punctuation point. Focus on it before or after a scene to comment on the significance of a character's sacrifice. Rather than an overt cross, let shadows create the form, or a vertical and a horizontal shape that are not joined but that form a cross when seen in perspective.

A character's outstretched arms can be a "crucified" pose.

OTHER EXAMPLES

The Passion of the Christ, Life of Brian, Spartacus, Kingdom of Heaven, Joan of Arc, El Topo.

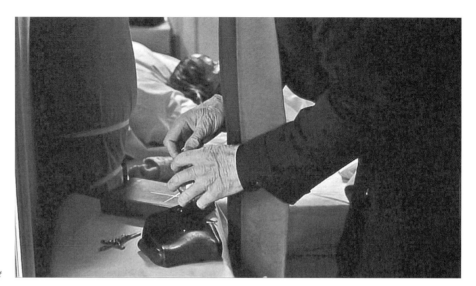

The Exorcist

The Graduate

18

DUALITY

WHAT IT MEANS

Humans are torn on the inside between different motives — the angel and the devil on our shoulders, whispering their dark-or-light, self-or-shadow urges into our ears. We are torn on the outside between the many choices life continually presents: the polarity of friendships and loves, the matching and mismatching of ourselves with others, work versus play. Symbols of duality strike a familiar and often troubling chord within our psyches.

IN HISTORY, MYTH, AND CONTEMPORARY TIMES

Influenced perhaps by the dualities of night and day, sun and moon, we tend to split our experience of the world into dualities: good and evil, hot and cold, war and peace, friend and foe, black and white, forward and back, past and present, life and death.

Most mythologies have a story about twins who usually end up as rivals, sometimes as friends. There were Jacob and Esau in the Old Testament, the Dogon Nummo twins, Mesoamerican twins Hunadu and Zbalanque, and Mesopotamian opposites Gilgamesh and Enkidu, who aren't actually related but after a fierce battle become best friends.

Carl Jung's anima and animus are, respectively, the male and female sides of the opposite gender.

One's doppelganger or ghost is usually an ill omen. In *Fight Club*, Brad Pitt is Edward Norton's doppelganger, living out the violent and confident parts of himself that he still represses.

IN MEDIA

In the silent classic *Metropolis*, an evil scientist builds a robot that looks just like the kindhearted human heroine; the robot twin leads rebellious workers to storm the city of the elites; the real woman saves the day. Even the machinery of the city is a duality, as seen in the chapter on architecture.

The Man in the Iron Mask is the story of French King Louis XIV and his hidden twin, rescued by the Musketeers.

Star Trek The Original Series: Season 3, Episode 15: Let That Be Your Last Battlefield

All Quiet on the Western Front

Dr. Jekyll and Mr. Hyde is a classic duality/twins story.

An episode in the first *Star Trek* TV series pits two men of different races on the same planet against each other in a lesson about the ridiculousness of prejudice: One man's face is black on the left and white on the right, and the other's is just the opposite.

In *Face-Off*, John Travolta and Nicholas Cage play an FBI agent and a terrorist with face-replacement operations and switched identities. The terrorist Castor Troy has a brother Pollux — named after the mythical twin brothers of Helen of Troy.

Harvey Dent and Batman become ill-fated twins in *The Dark Knight*.

A fragile butterfly on a brutal battlefield signals the duality of war in *All Quiet on the Western Front*.

Fish-out-of-water stories use duality and contrast to heighten emotional tension: streetwalker Julia Roberts shopping in Beverly Hills in *Pretty Woman*; street person Eddie Murphy in a financier's office in *Trading Places*; and bum Nick Nolte in *Down and Out in Beverly Hills*.

USE

+ To indicate an inner, psychological conflict.

+ To indicate two diverse ways of life: sophisticated vs. simple, ethical vs. depraved, solitary vs. gregarious.

+ To increase the conflict between characters or groups of characters.

+ To signal a deeper relationship between two seemingly diverse people or situations.

WRITTEN DESCRIPTIONS

Use linking words: similar, reflective, paired, joined, linked, and so on. Or use contrasting words: at odds, conflicting, opposing.

CINEMATIC TECHNIQUES

Use mirrors or other reflective surfaces to show both at once.

Film noir uses dark and light for dramatic effect on duality.

Change the color palette: *The English Patient* contrasts yellow desert sands and scorched skin with tubs and tanks of cool blue water.

OTHER EXAMPLES

There are twin witches in *Spirited Away*; *Heat* finds criminal Robert DeNiro and cop Al Pacino as mirrors of each other; Jeremy Irons in *Dead Ringers* and Bette Davis in *Dead Ringer* play troubled twins; *Frost/Nixon* illustrates the duality between those two men.

19

CULTURAL REFERENCES

WHAT IT MEANS

Community, shared background. Inclusivity for those in the know, exclusivity toward outsiders. It's a type of code and can be smug, lofty, or just fun.

IN MYTH, HISTORY, AND CONTEMPORARY TIMES

Symbols, images, and codes carry universal reference and are instinctual and intuitive. Cultural references are intellect-based and specific to a particular time, place, and people.

Back when educated people in Western civilization all learned the same things and shared a mythological and religious as well as political background, you could pepper your poetry, plays, and prose with references to Apollo's, Ezekiel's, or Boudica's chariot, Lethe's stream, Albion's shores, Gabriel's horn, the outer rings of hell, and so on. In Eastern civilization they'd know that Kwan Yin meant motherly compassion, to say "Farewell, my concubine" symbolized sacrificial romantic passion, and the man who danced with cowgirls was the blue-skinned god Krishna. It's a little different now, but every culture still has these marvelous stories that can be used when making media specific to that culture. Bridge Arts Media's logo

refers to Michelangelo's iconic image on the Sistine Chapel and calls to mind the spark of life and inspiration.

Artist: Darryl Sapien

Bridge Arts Media logo by Darryl Sapien

Using appropriate cultural references in your own stories can instantly hook your audience into all sorts of backstory and information. On the positive side, they can carry huge import; negative, they don't travel well across boundaries and can quickly become dated. Who'll think *Shrek II* is clever 50 years from now? (Who does now?)

Battle cries and political slogans use cultural references: "Forward the Light Brigade!", "Remember the Alamo!", "Where's the beef?", "It's the economy, stupid!", "Yes, we can!"

Generations identify themselves to each other with the passwords of cultural references: "23 Skidoo"; "Groovy, man"; "Gag me with a spoon … or pitchfork"; "Don't mess with the bull, you'll get the horns"; "Dude, don't freak out"; "Totally awesome"; "… not"; and so on. Most of those are from movies or music of a particular era.

And omg, I am so lol, so stop b4 it's 2 l8.

IN MEDIA

Windmills have become a potent symbol for nobly but futilely battling blind forces, a metaphor that traces back to Cervantes' novel *Don Quixote*, about a misguided knight tilting at windmills as though they were real enemies. At the end of the Oscar-winning film *Patton*, General Patton strides out into a field of windmills, symbolizing even this great man's inability to alter the force of politics overriding military prudence in World War II.

Patton

Bernardo Bertolucci's hauntingly brilliant film *The Conformist* stages the assassination of the fascist Conformist's former teacher as the assassination of Julius Caesar. Unlike noble Brutus' motives to save the Roman republic, the cowardly Italian Conformist is trying to save his own self-regard, with no real thought for Rome's heir, modern Italy.

Look at the examples in the "STEPS AND STAIRS," chapter, where the drama *The Untouchables* and the comedy *Naked Gun 2 1/2* both reference the Odessa Steps scene in the classic film *Battleship Potemkin*.

At the end of *Casablanca*, when Claude Rains' Captain Renault begins to side with Humphrey Bogart's Rick, he tosses the bottle of Vichy water into the trash. The French Vichy government had collaborated with the Nazis. By tossing the Vichy bottle, Renault is saying he is no longer going to collaborate with them, but will be switching his loyalty to Rick and Victor Laszlo and will now be fighting against the Nazis.

Many spiritual systems see life as a game, sometimes played by gods, sometimes by aliens, sometimes by blind fate. A famous scene from Ingmar Bergman's *The Seventh Seal* references this idea as Death and the knight-hero play chess on a beach.

The Conformist

The Seventh Seal

Bill & Ted's Excellent Adventure

Bill and Ted's Excellent Adventure references it with a foosball game, and *(500) Days of Summer* does it with Cupid playing chess with the heartbroken hero.

Tropic Thunder is nothing but cultural references, and it's ever so much fun. Every time we watch it, we try to find more references in dialogue, visuals, even the music. Like *Galaxy Quest*, however, it stands on its own as a fun and meaningful movie.

USE

+ When your intended audience will know the reference; otherwise you risk being totally misunderstood.

+ When you want to create an exotic world, use cultural references outside the scope of your audience, as Frank Herbert did in his *Dune* series of novels. The cultures he drew from were Arabian, Bedouin, and feudal European, which in '60s and '70s America were relatively unknown.

(500) Days of Summer

+ To layer a story with deeper significance for that smaller audience "in the know."

+ To finally make use of that English Lit, Comparative Mythology, or film school degree.

+ When you just want to have fun and bring your audience along with you.

WRITTEN DESCRIPTIONS

In literature you can be oblique with your references.

In scripts, be explicit.

CINEMATIC TECHNIQUES

Copy. As T.S. Eliot observed, "Immature poets imitate; mature poets steal." Of course you'll observe intellectual property rights, but by their very nature cultural references replicate a pattern, a pose, a lighting style.

Particularly in comedies, you can make good use of the double take when someone makes a cultural reference. Have another person respond with an expression that says, "Did you just say that?!"

Most of the time, since they are for the "In Crowd" and explaining it dilutes the fun of discovery, you don't want to give any on-screen acknowledgement that you've just made a cultural reference.

For the most part, it's best to have your visual cultural reference in the background or off to the side. You don't want to risk confusing the audience by highlighting something people don't get. Better to have a third of them spot it, go "Aha!" and love you for making them feel smart than to have two-thirds of them go "Huh?" and hate you for making them feel stupid.

Beware of product placement. Before the early '80s, media makers created ND (nondescript) items rather than use actual consumer products because you had to get all sorts of time-consuming and expensive clearances to show the real thing. Then along came "Product Placement," and the world changed. Suddenly manufacturers were paying to have their products show up in media. When is a Coke bottle not a Coke bottle? In *The Gods Must Be Crazy*, it's a symbol of so-called civilization and consumerism invading the remote and primitive world of the Kalahari Desert. Otherwise, it's just an advertisement for which Coke paid the producers. Of course, you can make statements with products, but they're so ubiquitous

in media these days that you have to go out of your way to bring emphasis to them, or your audience will figure you're just serving the product, not the story.

OTHER EXAMPLES

You needn't be Catholic to find *Dogma* amusing, or know Chinese mythology to thrill at *Crouching Tiger, Hidden Dragon*, but no doubt either background adds richness to the viewing experience.

Films like *Shrek, Scary Story, Tropic Thunder*, and the cult classic *Spinal Tap* work in great part because they're full of then-current cultural references.

Check out these other examples and what they're referencing and spoofing: *Dr. Strangelove* — Cold War political thrillers; Monty Python's *Life of Brian* — religious epics; *Young Frankenstein* — monster films; *Down with Love* — Doris Day and Rock Hudson comedies; *Galaxy Quest* — *Star Trek* and other sci-fi series; and all the films of spoofmeister Christopher Guest — real-life situations.

SITUATIONS & SYMBOLS

Some situations simply call out for symbols, images, and codes. The following chapters explore a number of these situations.

If you are creating any kind of media that reflects these concepts, your conscious use of visual metaphors can supply the communicative power to carry your theme, intent, character development, message, or call-to-action from you the creator to your audience.

These chapters can help you identify such situations, familiarize you with how the symbols work, and offer examples of their use in media.

You can then use the Index and the earlier chapters in this book to select and refine the symbols you will use to indicate these particular situations.

GOING NATIVE

WHAT IT MEANS

Cutting ties with one's own people; rejection of one's own culture.

A shift in loyalty; unpredictability; rebelliousness.

Depending on how the native culture is portrayed, Going Native can be either a descent or an ascent.

Self-sacrifice in favor of a higher ideal; descent into a darker realm.

IN HISTORY, MYTH, AND CONTEMPORARY TIMES

This type of character transformation differs from initiation because the person is coming from the outside into a significantly different social system. Typically, this involves a lone individual entering an unfamiliar society or culture.

Thematically, Going Native is similar to the idea that we are here in exile from heaven, paradise, a golden era, a faraway star system, and so on — all of which may be explanations of our psychological sense of isolation, something that first strikes us when as young children we realize that the world isn't all about us.

It is a story that has been told and retold throughout time, probably from back when the first hunter wandered away from his home tribe, met some new people, and decided he liked it there better.

Warriors throughout the ages have stayed in the countries they invaded or brought home war brides, both of which provide situations for Going Native stories.

During the European colonial era, a typical sign was the Brits-below-the-tropics syndrome: the "propah" Englishman with the meticulous regimental uniform coat or formal dinner jacket above the waist, and the casual sarong and bare feet below the waist. The sexual symbolism there is fairly obvious.

A British officer in World War I tells one of the most famous Going Native stories in his autobiography, *Seven Pillars of Wisdom*. T.E. Lawrence was also known as Lawrence of Arabia.

The hero of Going Native stories is usually male, though the act of acceptance and nonviolent assimilation is more typically thought of as female. In the modern world, where more women explore, go on military campaigns, and are in foreign situations, you have more opportunities for them to star in Going Native stories.

IN MEDIA

Going Native is the theme of an all-time favorite movie, *Avatar*. Like many explorers of frontiers, Marine Jake Sully steps into a wondrous new world and is enchanted by the people and the environment. Torn by conflicting loyalties, he finds a growing acceptance by the Na'vi as his acceptance of them deepens.

The hero often brings new insights and skills to the so-called natives, no matter what their current level of sophistication. Two prime examples are Lawrence of Arabia unifying the already fierce desert tribes during World War I to make them even more effective fighters, and the Tom Cruise character bringing classic warfare strategy to the already superb Samurai warriors in *The Last Samurai*.

Rather than Going Native willingly, sometimes the hero is forced into the situation — captured, for instance — but then gradually learns to respect, accept, and excel in the locals' ways, as in *A Man Called Horse*.

Going Native often incurs a serious backlash from the hero's original culture. In *Apocalypse Now*, Captain Willard is sent upriver to terminate the command of Colonel Kurtz because the colonel went native in a really dark way. In *The Last Samurai*, Tom Cruise's American military advisor Nathan Algren disobeys orders and helps remaining Samurai warriors fight against the destruction of what is portrayed as their noble tradition; Algren then has to face fierce counterattacks. Jake Sully's defection to the Na'vi in *Avatar* escalates the corporate mercenaries' attacks and triggers a personal vendetta against Jake by Colonel Quaritch.

Because drama depends on contrast, showing others who have not gone native can be an effective way to show what the hero is giving up, as well as what his punishments might be for doing so. In *Apocalypse Now Redux*, Captain Willard and the men meet the French plantation family who did not go native. Willard is invited to a dinner replete with crystal and china, formal dinner wear, and sophisticated conversation and manners. He's also enticed into a romantic interlude with a lovely and gracious Frenchwoman. The contrast between that and Colonel Kurtz' compound is dramatic. The award-winning *Indochine* is another example of the contrast between Going Native and not.

SPECIFIC SYMBOLS

A single object merging into something bigger: one drop of water into a pool of water, a lone animal into a herd or flock, a single human into a crowd.

The protagonist putting on the clothing, makeup, hairstyle, or "look" of the locals.

The hero doing something distinctly local that he had previously avoided: drink, dance, romance, etc.

USE

+ To make statements about personal, social, political, and species attitudes and ways of life. In the beginning of *Apocalypse Now*, the general's speech about good and evil and the conflict in every man's heart is the key theme of the movie. *Avatar*'s Going Native theme comments on the tendency of imperial power to take what it wants regardless of the wishes and the welfare of the locals.

+ To take a character in an arc from unthinking acceptance to an awakened conscience.

+ As the barrier to a love story; then the hero's acceptance into the beloved's culture resonates with their union.

WRITTEN DESCRIPTIONS

Because the concept is about leaving one system and joining another, write that with distinct specificity: "He tears away from the arms holding him back and races across the battlefield into the arms of the enemy, his new comrades."

When the hero is finally accepted by the community, have some token that symbolizes the acceptance and that we have seen him reject before, or that has been withheld from him. At the moment of acceptance, have a pause and give your hero — and your audience — a chance to reflect on the meaning. Then tell us specifically how it is given to him, or how he picks it up or puts it on, to indicate his emotion at that time, which could be rebellious, relieved, cautious, confident.

Use words like "alone," "solitary," "isolated," "apart" to describe the hero before his defection and acceptance. Afterwards, use words such as "included," "accepted," "linked," "assimilated."

CINEMATIC TECHNIQUES

Because the symbolism is about a lone individual becoming assimilated into an alien culture, you'll want to show that individual moving/walking/riding/flying in to join a group of the locals. The visual can be like a drop of water falling into a pool of water, or like a single bird joining a flock.

Clothes, hairstyles, makeup, language — all can signal that the hero is taking on a new identity. Isolate the five moments when the hero finally puts on the new identity:

1. Show the hesitancy just before he crosses that line.

2. Show him doing it.

3. Give him at least a brief quiet time to reflect on it.

4. Show the reactions of the natives to his actions.

5. Not too long after that, show the reactions of his original culture to his defection and/or what he now does differently since he has defected.

In *The Last Samurai* there is a sequence of Cruise's Algren being formally dressed in Samurai armor. In *Tropic Thunder* Ben Stiller does a hilarious job of Going Native.

OTHER EXAMPLES

District 9, Dances with Wolves, Pocahontas, The Emerald Forest, The Man Who Would Be King, Alien Nation, Farewell to the King, Little Big Man, Tarzan, The Last of the Mohicans, Robinson Crusoe, John Carter of Mars.

SEX, LOVE, & ROMANCE

WHAT IT MEANS

Along with volcanoes and tsunamis, sex and love are among nature's most powerful, overwhelming, and radically transformative effects. Love, lust, affection, power plays, reproduction, surrender, ecstasy, commerce, degradation, consolation, the mercy boff, persuasion, deception, betrayal, the death of love … the entire gamut of human experience can be reflected in sex. Add love and romance and you have yearning, delight, and poetic inspiration. For the lucky ones, sex, love, and romance can become transformative and enlightening.

As poetry expresses in a few words the numinous potency of our awareness of life, so too can symbolic illustrations of sex, love, and romance be turned into powerful poetry.

IN HISTORY, MYTH, AND CONTEMPORARY TIMES

The creation myths of many cultures begin with sex, typically a father sky and mother earth, though sometimes it's a solitary act, such as the Milky Way being the result of a deity's self-pleasuring. Sex, love, and romance are a regular part of many deities' existence, among themselves and with mere mortals. Sometimes the immortal sex partners aren't human at all; Greek king-god Zeus surely holds

a record for shape-shifting for his romantic trysts: a bull, a swan, a shower of gold, etc.

The Hindu temple of Kuharajo is replete with carvings of various gymnastic sexual positions. Some say it's a just a visual manual for lovemaking; mystics say it's a wiring diagram for enlightenment — put this chakra point over that one, connect these three, and so on.

Doomed Norse and Celtic lovers Siegfried and Brunhilde and Tristan and Isolde are often shown languishing with limbs entwined, fully clothed but obviously enraptured and felled by passion — the emotion indicated by the poses and the looks as well as attending symbols, be they rings of fire, sailing ships, cliffs for hurling oneself from, or swords and armor set aside in the heat of passion.

Fairy tales often have sexual innuendoes hidden throughout: magic kisses that awaken the sleeper (*Sleeping Beauty*), rings of fire or glass coffins surrounding a maiden (Brunhilde and *Snow White*), tall towers and long hair (*Rapunzel*), tempting apples and anatomically suggestive glass slippers (*Cinderella*).

Bernini's white marble statue of Saint Teresa of Avila surely depicts romantic if not downright sexual ecstasy. The arrow held by the Cupid-Eros angel standing over her and lifting part of her garment can certainly be read as phallic. The moment is taken from her writings, describing a spiritually transcendent event. The connection between sexual and spiritual communion and illumination is deeply embedded in many mystical traditions, be it the springtime mating of stand-ins for the gods, Krishna dancing with the Gopi cow-girls, or Christ and his bride the Church.

Though in some cultures women and sometimes men as well are almost completely covered head to toe, in others near-naked is everyday attire. Clothing can thus say worlds about a person's and a culture's attitudes toward sex and romance. It can also hide attitudes and actions, such as sexy outfits beneath a burka or garter belts under a pinstripe suit.

Depending on the time and culture, same-sex love often has to rely on secret signals, symbols, and codes. Whether a style of clothing, a mannerism, or a phrase, these codes open doors to an otherwise forbidden realm.

IN MEDIA

Cultural mores have influenced what gets shown in media since humans began drawing on cave walls. Classical Greco-Roman art is resplendent with nudes. Middle Ages Greek and Italian art featured buttoned-up pious churchgoers. In Victorian England, piano legs were considered too sexy for viewing, much less real women's ankles; less than a hundred years later Britain led the fashion world with miniskirts. Time isn't the only divider of what's appropriate; witness the severe clothing restrictions in many strict religious cultures, even when surrounded by anything-goes modernism. In the 1960s and 1970s, American films were often shot two ways, the European version being more sexually explicit.

In *Apocalypse Now*, when Captain Willard and the boat crew reach a U.S. military base preparing for a visit by Playboy Bunnies, they find the waterside stage decorated with upright missiles (phallic symbols) and banks of lights in half-circles (breast symbols). In contrast to that rocking, raunchy sexual sequence, in *Apocalypse Now Redux* when Captain Willard makes love with the French plantation woman, the tone is genteel, romantic, and yearning, filled with classical music, fine furnishings, billowing fabric, and soft lighting. Both sequences are about putting body parts together, but the feel is radically different because of the visuals and pacing.

In the Realm of Senses and *Last Tango in Paris* are both highly erotically charged films that are quite explicit without being X-rated. They're excellent examples of creating the cloistering, consuming nature of sexual obsession by increasingly narrowing the confines of the lovers' world.

Miss Pettigrew Lives for a Day has many varieties of love, lust, and sexual manipulation going on, all expressed in different ways with different types of clothes, food, and actions. *Love Actually* is an excellent example of love and sex in many varieties. In the main love triangle, the husband gives his secretary and potential fling a heart necklace and gives his wife a music CD, symbolizing his differing attitudes toward them.

Two very effective pieces of media that can send people into swoons of desire are Richard Wagner's *Liebestod* (love-death) from his opera *Tristan and Isolde* and Maurice Ravel's orchestral piece *Bolero*, which became the theme song for the 1979 movie about erotic desire, *10*. Both works use sustained tension and specific pacing to create the mood. Listen to this music for excellent patterns of how to pace your sentences, your camera moves, your editing cuts.

Attitudes about sex are cyclic. For differing uses of symbols, images, and codes to indicate same-sex love and how attitudes change over time, watch *Maurice*, the wrestling scene in *Women in Love*, *Brideshead Revisited*, *In and Out*, and the director's cut of *Lawrence of Arabia*. In the 1920s and 1930s, violets symbolized lesbian love, and the gender preference of women wearing men's attire was highly suspect. In the 1930s Paris supposedly forbade Marlene Dietrich to appear in public in slacks — or perhaps it was just a studio publicity stunt. For various treatments of that type of sex and love, watch the progression of the relationship between Xena and Gabrielle in the mid-1990s TV series *Xena: Warrior Princess* versus *The L Word* series, *Boys on the Side*, *Bound*, and *The Hunger*.

SPECIFIC SYMBOLS

Underwear — in various stages of presence or absence. Clark Gable and Marlon Brando made undershirts really sexy. Madonna made underwear outerwear. Context matters: Underwear twirling on the ceiling fan says something quite different from underwear neatly folded in a drawer. Different styles of underwear communicate different kinds of sex and love: In *Fatal Attraction* the good wife wore modest white cotton panties; the dangerous lover wore scanty lace lingerie, if any at all.

Fire — as noted in that chapter. Deepa Mehta's film *Fire* has excellent examples of the different types of loving and sexual connections centered around different types of fire. Mythic Norse hero Siegfried must pass through a ring of fire to claim the warrior princess Brunhilde by waking her with a kiss. But first he thoughtfully removes her armor … riiight.

Water — as noted in that chapter. In *Howard's End* Helena Bonham Carter meets a young man on a rainy day when he gets soaked following her home to retrieve his umbrella. Later when he's married they go rowing on a stream, start kissing and rocking the boat, and obviously end up having sex as evidenced by the baby born nine months later. Ralph Fiennes and Kristin Scott-Thomas sit together in a bathtub after making love for the first time in *The English Patient*. A rain-drenched kiss in *Streets of Fire* brings former lovers Diane Lane and Michael Pare back together, for a while. The first romantic kiss in *Australia* happens during the first rainstorm of the monsoon season. The sheen of perspiration is often a cue for sexual exertion.

Air — In times and cultures where showing physical contact between a couple is forbidden, the camera often swings out a window to the open sky to indicate wider horizons, limitless possibilities, and freedom from old ways. Showing the sun coming up through the same window in the same room says they've been in bed together all night, even if they aren't both still in the room. The balloons in *Up* are colorful, tender symbols of the old man's love for both his adored, departed wife and their mutual sense of adventure.

Swinging — the playground kind (but it's interesting that acknowledged, mutual extramarital affairs are called "swinging"). Girls on swings feature in many classical works of art, as well as in *The Thin Red Line*. The up-and-down gliding of swinging easily equates to sex, just as the giddiness and breathtaking sense of weightlessness equate to falling in love.

Sensual food — from bubbly champagne, to caviar and oysters, to the blatant fig-eating scene in *Women in Love*, culinary references can say delicious indulgence on many levels. Lolita's lollipop glistens with nymphet seduction. Ice cubes were never the same after *Nine 1/2 Weeks*. Chocolate contains oxytocin, the feel-good bonding hormone, so a babe reclining on a sofa eating bonbons and petting a perfumed Pekingese is probably up to more than just relaxing. The effects of chocolate sustain the entire film *Chocolat*.

Disheveled hair and clothes — particularly when contrasted to a formerly neat appearance. The popularity of the bedhead look is doubtless its implication of having just risen from a sexual spree.

USE

+ To show a deepening intimacy or commitment between characters.
+ To show a sexual or sensual connection.
+ To show the yearning for some kind of connection.
+ To show out-of-control emotions, or emotions too much under control.
+ To indicate the crossing of a no-going-back line.
+ To show danger, devastation, or destruction via sexual threat or actual assault.
+ To parallel the breaking of an individual's or people's spirit — rape as a weapon of war.

WRITTEN DESCRIPTIONS

Generally speaking, the more explicit the descriptions, the less literary the piece. Good writers can heat up a scene without ever using a specific body-part word. Use sense words such as feasting, tasting, engulfing, consuming, breathless, heart-racing, pulsing, etc.

Select just one or two symbols or images and stick with those for internal consistency. Too many verbal and visual innuendoes border on comedy or porn.

A break in the pace of the story with paragraph spaces, asterisks, or a new chapter can indicate a sexual interlude.

CINEMATIC TECHNIQUES

To be symbolic rather than explicit as in actual pornography or the likes of *Grand Theft Auto*, keep in mind what creates sexual and romantic tension: yearning. Move in closer to the "target," — a pair of luscious lips, a hand, a lock of hair — but stop just short of contact. Sustain that visual pause to raise the tension before completing contact. Or stop before visible contact; it all depends on the style and plot of your story.

To indicate sex about to happen, let the characters move down out of frame, or turn the lens away from the characters. Or send then toward a bedroom like Rhett carrying Scarlet up that grand staircase in *Gone with the Wind*.

Down with Love is replete with sexual symbolism and spoofs on same, as is *Austin Powers: International Man of Mystery*. Both use the placement of props, camera angles, and intercutting to make visual sexual jokes.

Sexual charge and tension are created by friction, literally as well as imaginatively. If you think of a seduction scene like a piece of music, you'll want it to begin tentatively, then move to slow and languid caresses, then increase the pace of actions-cuts-angles to a crescendo, a pause, and then a relaxation. Listen to the musical pieces suggested above for ideas on pacing.

OTHER EXAMPLES

Gustav Klimpt's painting *The Kiss*; *Dr. Jekyll and Mr. Hyde*; *Crouching Tiger, Hidden Dragon*; *Atonement*; *In Harm's Way*; *Secretary*; *Mrs. Brown*; *Kama Sutra*; *Raise the Red Lantern*.

+ 2 3 +

WEAPONS, WOUNDS, & DEATHS

WHAT IT MEANS

Live by the sword, die by the sword.

Karma.

As ye sow, so shall ye reap.

Poetic justice.

IN HISTORY, MYTH, AND CONTEMPORARY TIMES

It's a mythic-esoteric rule that the only thing that can heal you is the thing that caused your wound. It's the same principle as vaccinations and homeopathy, but taken too far it can lead to stalking and black magic.

Horribly wounded by decapitation, the Hindu god Ganesh gets an elephant head to replace his human one. He's also missing a tusk. Among his many symbolisms, he is embraced as a remover of obstacles, a wise one, and as someone who was badly wounded but carries on and does remarkably well, with good spirits. He is thus often an icon for people in recovery.

King Amfortas of the Holy Grail myths has one of the most famous wounds in history. He's hurt in his thigh, which is usually interpreted as a sexual wound that has made him impotent and infertile, hence standing for the entire kingdom going into decline.

In mystic Christian iconography, Saint George carries a lance and pierces the dragon through the throat, while Saint Michael wields a sword and pierces the dragon in the heart. Each wound symbolizes a different approach to victory: the intellect (throat) and the emotions (heart).

As though reflecting humanity, many gods are wounded: Norse god Odin is missing an eye, Greco-Roman toolmaker god Hephaestus-Vulcan is lame, and many cultures sacrifice their gods in rather grim rituals, from crucifixions to ripping out hearts to tearing them limb from limb. Many of the gods revive in time for the next season's sacrifice, but weapons, wounds, and deaths still say worlds about a culture's world view.

Death by animal can reveal much about characters or situations: that they've fatally ignored the natural world, that they were cruel to animals or too kind and therefore stupid about animals, that nature is heedless of man, or that man is helpless against nature.

IN MEDIA

The Viking funeral is a big deal, mythically speaking. Laying the dead warrior on a boat with his sword, his dog, and perhaps some other valued belongings, and then setting the boat on fire and pushing it out to sea … that's mythic. *Patriot Games* plays a version of this when villain Sean Bean dies on a fiery boat in a fight with hero Harrison Ford.

In Baz Lurhman's *Australia*, the bad guy Fletcher kills a rancher by hurling a ceremonial Aborigine spear through him and spreading the rumor that an Abo elder did it. At the end of the film, Fletcher is killed by that very same Aborigine elder protecting his grandson. The weapon of death is a piece of metal torn from Fletcher's own water tank and hurled like a spear to kill him the same way he had killed the rancher. The double parallels make the symbolism quite powerful. Additionally, the boy the elder is protecting is Fletcher's mixed-race son.

In *The Professional*, Jean Reno's assassin has been shot by Gary Oldman's corrupt DEA agent. As Oldman mocks him, the dying Reno hands him the "gift" of a grenade pin – symbol of instant inescapable death — and reveals he's wearing a vest full of explosives. Boom! It's a fitting end for both men whose lives had been about blowing apart other people's lives, deservedly or not. I knew a producer who used to wear a grenade pin on a string of pearls the first day of a film shoot; she said that symbol of combat readiness typically gained an immediate respect from the guys on her crew.

Colonel Kurtz in *Apocalypse Now* has gone native in a really dark way, condoning mayhem and murder, festooning trees with dead bodies, and planting severed heads all around his compound. It makes perfect story sense that Captain Willard assassinates Kurtz in the same way and at the same time that Kurtz' local minions sacrifice a bull in a frenzied traditional ceremony. A large machete to the back of the neck ends both lives. (See also "Going Native.")

Egotistical two-timing gangster Joe Pantoliano dies a vivid death in the lesbo-mafia romp *Bound*: His girlfriend (who's fallen in love with another woman) shoots him in a pool of white paint and watches the blood seep out in crimson counterpoint.

Inglourious Basterds uses exaggerated symbols such as Brad Pitt's giant bowie knife and the Jewish boy's baseball bat, playing respectively on American frontier lore and America's love for the wholesome sport of baseball. The baseball bat is a reverse reference in *The Untouchables*, when De Niro's Capone uses the iconic sports symbol to beat an errant minion to death.

Quieter deaths include poison, strangling, suffocation. My book *INNER DRIVES* offers examples of appropriate wounds and deaths to go along with a character's Center of Motivation/chakra.

D.H. Lawrence uses two forms of death by water in *Women in Love*. In the beginning of the story a bride and groom are drowned, she having pulled him into the depths; Lawrence likens it to the emotional female destroying the male. Later the bride's brother walks into an icy death on a skiing trip, having been deprived of love and emotional warmth.

Jack in *Titanic* drowns in the icy waters, rather than perishing on the ship being crushed by falling chandeliers, or trampled by the panicked crowd. Water symbolizes the emotions, so it is a perfect death for him, who brought emotional and sexual awakening to Rose.

Horror films and games are chock full of all sorts of imaginative and usually gory weapons, wounds, and deaths. They're much more effective if they match the personality or actions of the character and if there is a setup before the payoff of the wounding or death. However, the deaths in the *Alien* movies, literally from within as well as without, were just plain awful. What character deserved any of that, really?

SPECIFIC SYMBOLS

Projectiles; sharp objects.

Swords are esoterically a tool of the mind, cutting through deception and confusion.

Weapon parts: grenade pins, bullets, crosshairs.

Exotic weapons demand extra alertness: chakram (*Xena*), Ninja stars, blow darts, light sabers (*Star Wars*), ray guns (*District 9*).

Skull and crossbones, biohazard signs = poison, death; circle with slash = forbidden.

Scars.

Red apples = forbidden poisonous fruit (Garden of Eden, *Snow White*).

USE

+ To mete out justice or revenge to the bad guys.

+ To emphasize the retributive actions and results of fate, karma, or local laws.

+ To bookend your story.

+ To illustrate a philosophy of existence.

+ To give your protagonist a rousing, well-deserved victory over the antagonist.

WRITTEN DESCRIPTIONS

To make a wound or death symbolic, you need a setup, such as in *Australia* with the spear, or as in *Die Hard 2: Die Harder* with the fiery airplane crash, which the bad guys threaten to do to a full passenger plane.

If it's been a long time since your audience has witnessed the setup, give them a reminder. In *Australia*, Fletcher is skewered by the makeshift spear, just as he had skewered Lord Ashley with the Aborigine spear. Use the same word(s) somewhere in your description to make clear the connection.

Being hoisted by one's own petard is a great story turn, where someone's deadly intent for others wounds or kills him or her instead. The poisoner sips from the wrong glass, the deadly germs escape too soon, the attacker's gun is pointing the wrong way in the struggle, the pursuer slips to her own death. If you've done your setup or foreshadowing well enough, you shouldn't have to point out the irony just then, but someone can always comment later: Oh, he missed the train (fell under it trying to kill me), she ate something that disagreed with her (the poison she meant for me), etc.

For imaginative and gruesome deaths, check out hagiographies, the lives and deaths of saints.

CINEMATIC TECHNIQUES

Draw the audience's attention to the wound or weapon for the setup. A character could be either dismissive or fearful of the item. Show it again before the death to heighten the tension. Depending on the type of weapon or death, intercutting can be very effective.

Cut between your characters' eyes and their points of view of the weapon or danger to signal their growing awareness of peril.

What happens after a weapon is used can speak volumes about the character's attitude toward the whole thing. After assassinating

Apocalypse Now's Colonel Kurtz with the machete, Captain Willard drops the bloody thing before the native crowd and walks away from the whole situation; he will not follow Kurtz into that heart of darkness.

OTHER EXAMPLES

Raiders of the Lost Ark: At the end, the Nazis are fried by the power of the object they caused so much death and mayhem to obtain. Brokenhearted Colin Firth dying of a heart attack in *A Single Man*. The voracious beetles in *The Mummy*. The unstoppable machine *The Terminator* being crushed by a machine. The *Nightmare on Elm Street* and *Friday the 13*th series are rich with imaginative deaths.

EXERCISES

Learning to consciously recognize and interpret symbols, images, and codes is an admirable thing. Learning to consciously create them is entirely another thing, just as appreciating music, poetry, or architecture is quite another thing from being able to create real works of art in those media. Here are some exercises that can make you more adept at the selection and use of symbols.

Now you see it, now you see it again. For each chapter in this book, observe various media for a week and see how many examples of that symbol or image you can find. One day do novels, the next day TV series, then billboards, movies, magazine ads, games, logos, etc.

See it, feel it, hear it. Some people naturally have a condition called synesthesia, where their brain mixes their senses and they can "taste" colors, "feel" sounds, etc. Some entertainment technology matches colors to sounds, as in concert light shows. Act as if you have this ability and imagine what color certain shapes would be. Assign a musical note or chord to specific shapes so that when you see a circle, you hum that chord; when you note a triangle, you hum the chord for that shape. It's easy to put feelings to music; try the harder approach and put feelings to a certain letter, animal, tree, architectural detail, something atypical.

Shifting symbols within a scene. Select a symbol in one of your own stories, or one in a particular novel, movie, or game. What does that symbol represent? Refer to the Index and identify the symbol as an Emotion, Situation, or Concept. Within those categories, select another symbol that represents the same Emotion, Situation, or Concept and rewrite a scene using that symbol instead of the original one.

For example, in the story you selected, the Concept of Sacrifice may be represented by blood. For your rewrite select Fire, or a Leap, or Descending Stairs, and build that symbolism into the scene instead of Fire.

This ability to shift symbols can be exceptionally helpful in film-making where you often face a situation in financing or during shooting that makes your original idea difficult to accomplish. Being able to express the same meaning with a different symbol keeps your intent intact.

Shifting symbols over time. As cultural norms change, the symbols related to them change. Pick something that has undergone a change in public opinion and find two or three media examples from each phase of the change.

Smoking: from sophisticated to a weakness to rebellious and retro.

Unintended pregnancies and out-of-wedlock children: from a deadly scandal to daringly rebellious to a common fact.

Interracial marriage, intercultural marriage, inter-religious marriage, same-sex marriage.

Women's rights and freedoms, in different cultures.

Implicit to explicit. Read Vladimir Nabokov's novel *Lolita*, then watch the 1962 film, then the 1997 film. Compare the treatment of the sexual encounters in the three versions. Which is more explicit? Which do you find more powerful and why?

Compare the torrid sexual tension in *Double Indemnity* with that in *Body Heat*. Which man was more besotted? Which couple had the hotter sex? How do you know?

Spotting symbols. Watch Bertolucci's classic film *The Conformist* before watching the DVD's Special Features. See how many different symbols and images you can identify. Some of them are noted in this book, many others are not. After you have made your list, watch the Special Features section about the symbolism and see how many you found.

An artist's consistency, or not. Watch Bertolucci's *The Last Emperor* and see how many symbols and images he uses in this film that are similar to those in *The Conformist*: architecture, blocking, contrasts, cultural confinement, etc.

Watch Bertolucci's *Last Tango in Paris*. How many times did Bertolucci use symbols and images now familiar to you? Can you find three to five new ones? Do this with the works of some of your other favorite writers and directors.

As a writer or director, what would your favorite symbols be for falling in love, doomed to die, freedom? Have you been recycling symbols in your work?

Imagery across cultures. *Last Tango in Paris* came out in 1972 and *In the Realm of the Senses* in 1976. The former is European and the latter Japanese; both deal with sexual obsession, both are rated NC-17, and both caused a huge sensation when they debuted. Compare and contrast the two films for the use of symbols and imagery.

Animal attraction. Watch *The Golden Compass*, or better yet read Philip Pullman's entire *His Dark Materials* trilogy, then select your own daemon according to the world of that story, keeping in mind affinities or antagonisms with daemons of the existing characters. In other words, if you selected a chimp, would you be in competition or collaboration with Nicole Kidman and her golden spider monkey?

Show, don't tell. Use sign language, not the official one that spells out words with letters, but the kind aliens use on first contact. How do you indicate with your hands, eyes, and expressions various things, feelings, concepts?

Code talkers. Make up a code and use it among a couple of friends. See if others can figure it out. And no, texting abbreviations do not count!

Leitmotif. Select a Richard Wagner opera. Read an overview or analysis, read the actual libretto, listen to the music, and identify the leitmotif or phrase of music that belongs to each character. *Siegfried* is an excellent one for this exercise.

Then select the soundtrack from a movie and identify the motifs for various characters. Working with another person, see if you can identify who's on screen or what's going on just by listening to the music and sound. Obviously sometimes dialogue will tell you, but often a sequence begins with sound and music, not dialogue.

Think how you can transfer this concept of a unique leitmotif for each character to your own visual media.

They've got your number. Someone probably teaches college courses on the *Lost* TV series, in both the media and mathematics departments. Identify the series of numbers that unlocked the vault, that were the winning number on Hurley's lottery ticket, that were all over the cave … and where else? Why those numbers? Before

the mystery was solved, what did you think they meant, or stood for?

Spoof this. *Inglourious Basterds*: How many exaggerated symbols can you identify, including the characteristic, motif, or fact to which they refer? The baseball bat as weapon, for example, plays on America's love for the wholesome sport; the fact that it is used to beat Nazis to death indicates that America is going to terrorize and then beat the Nazis into bloody submission.

Choose your weapons. After you've read the chapter on Weapons, Wounds, and Deaths, go through each chapter on symbols and:

1. find a media incident reflecting that symbol as a means of wounds or deaths. For Architecture it could involve being killed by a falling building or falling off a building. Then:

2. make up a new one. For Architecture it might be forcing someone to eat lead paint or swallow nails (eewww), or tying them between two sides of an opening drawbridge (ow!).

CONCLUSION

The world is already over the threshold of a major change in the way we gather, process, and disseminate information. Yet for the most part our brains still work the same way they have for thousands of years.

Our written and spoken communications can span the globe in seconds, but each individual, each culture, and each interest group will process such communication through a distinct set of identifiers and interpretations. One very effective way past these barriers is to use visuals. Some are so universal as to be understood anywhere by anyone. Others require some cultural background. As a media creator, you can make good use of the wide range of symbols, images, and codes to enhance your meaning and enrich your stories, be they novels, movies, TV, games, marketing, plays, or political campaigns.

I hope you find this collection of visual communication devices of great value in your work as an artist, as a crafter of stories, and as an individual transmitting your own spin on the timeless themes and archetypes to the rest of us, whether for entertainment, education, or enlightenment.

index

Sure, there are certain images that say scary (skeletons and vicious beasts), and some that say warm and fuzzy (puppies and kittens). But so much of what makes symbols and images work is their context. Play something up blatantly and it becomes melodrama. The same symbol done subtly becomes drama. Juxtapose it with the unexpected and you can get comedy. All from the same symbol. Another aspect of symbolism in media is people's reaction to the symbol. Religious symbols in particular carry different meanings depending on the reception they receive: inspiration, oppression, scorn, comfort, etc. One of the best examples is the Hindu symbol for good luck that became the Nazi swastika.

It would be wonderful if we could just section off the story genres into neat categories such as action-adventure, romantic comedy, horror, sci-fi, and drama, and then place certain symbols distinctly in those categories. That way, whenever we wanted to do a specific genre story, we could just pull out those same symbols and, voila! But down that road lies stereotyping, redundancy, and unimaginative filmmaking.

It is depths and layers that make characters and stories so compelling. Graciousness and charm carry totally different meanings depending on whether a character is being, say, compassionate or cynical. Use a symbol one way in the beginning of a heroine's journey, another way in the middle, and yet again a different way at the end, and you can show in exterior form something about her interior shifts. Playing against stereotypes with symbols can deepen the meaning of your story. A pirate's flag of the skull and crossbones (danger, poison, death) takes on extra layers if your pirate is a member of a secret philosophical society that reveres the same figure as symbolic of the life of the body (thighbone marrow creates red blood cells) and the life of the mind (the brain in the skull). Taking your characters and your audience through the journey of discovering the many layers of your symbols, images, and codes will make your stories all the more fascinating.

This index categorizes the symbols and images found throughout this book according to three levels of storycraft: personal emotions, social and environmental situations, and high concepts. Each level is typically larger in reach and influence than the one before it, though in the best stories the emotions of the individual drive everything, from the inside out.

Personal Emotions are what your characters experience inside as they go through the story. It's also what you want your audience to experience as we read your book, watch your film, play your game, see your ad, or listen to your campaign speech. This is the complex compilation of sad, glad, mad, and other emotions that makes up human psychology.

This section is where you'll look to find something that will reveal your characters, will show them changing, will explain their hopes and fears, strengths and weaknesses.

Social and Environmental Situations are the external barriers, conflicts, and struggles your hero must overcome, such as war, family strife, political oppression, and natural disasters. They are also the rewards of having done so, such as peace, material abundance, community bonding.

You know how you're always told to make the journey difficult for your hero? Layering your scenes with symbols and images that do so can create deliciously complex stories that have an impact on many levels.

Concepts are more abstract but are at the core of all good stories. The mythic theme of your story — unless it's just a silly comedy (and there's nothing wrong with that) or a slasher film with no redeeming social value (not necessarily anything wrong with that either) — will usually contain an idea that is universal and either inspires us or warns us away from something.

We're all living, breathing, fighting, and dying for something. Or certainly your characters should be; otherwise they'll be deadly boring. How do you show the concepts of freedom, equality, loyalty, spiritual aspiration? This is where symbols and images come to the rescue and plug your audience into those universal streams of meaning and make your media about more than just the plot line.

A classic example of combining all three aspects of emotional, situational, and conceptual symbolism comes from the ancient Greeks. Some of the bloodiest vengeance-driven stories ever concocted revolve around the Greek House of Atreus, a clan who tended to serve each other — for dinner. These cautionary tales carry the emotions of greed, jealousy, lust, ambition, and vengeance, but at the very end they rise to uphold and embrace the concepts of forgiveness and rational thought.

Emotions = Cauldron. The boiling cauldron used to cook up the Atreus relatives symbolizes the boiling emotions of scorn, lust, and jealousy barely contained in the crucible of the cursed family.

Situation = Crossroads. As a young man, Oedipus — separated from his Atreus-lineage parents as a baby so he wouldn't fulfill the prophecy that he'd kill his father and marry his mother — kills a man at a crossroads who turns out to be his true father, an event that changes everyone's lives.

Concept = Blindness. Oedipus blinds himself out of sorrow and regret, and wanders for years before receiving absolution. His blindness represents blind Fate, which to the Greeks was inescapable. No matter what you did, where you ran, or how you hid, Fate would find you out. It was the early version of "stuff happens." In some versions of the myth, Oedipus is healed by the goddess Athena, who wears her helmet pushed back on her head so it looks like she has two sets of eyes: one for the earthly world and one for the spiritual realm. Many spiritual disciplines have a version of this concept of opening your eyes to higher truths, the scales falling from your eyes: "I was blind, but now I see."

For your story, select a main symbol for each of these categories. If you can use the same one in different ways in different categories, all the better.

Beside each emotion, situation, and concept are the chapters containing detailed information. Further specifics within a chapter follow the chapter's title: for example, Connections: Anatomy — hands.

EMOTIONS AND ATTRIBUTES

+ Adventurous: Astronomy. Color — red, metallics, blue. Earth — wide open spaces. The Leap. Steps and Stairs.

+ Ambition: Anatomy — feet. Fire. The Leap. Steps and Stairs.

+ Angry: Anatomy — hands, clenched. Color — red, orange. Fire. The Leap.

+ Compassion: Anatomy — heart. Color — red. Crosses. Cultural References.

+ Courage: Anatomy — heart. Animals — lion. Color — red. Crosses. Fire. The Leap.

+ Cowardice: Animals — mouse. Color — yellow. Duality. Numbers — 0.

+ Crafty, Wily: Animals — fox, serpent. Color — orange. Cultural References. Duality.

+ Friendly: Anatomy — hands, open. Color — green. Cultural References.

+ Geekiness: Anatomy — head. Astronomy. Cultural References. Numbers.

+ General Emotions and Attributes: Astronomy and Astrology. Chakras. Clothes. Water.

+ Generous — Anatomy — hands, open. Color — green, gold. Earth — fertile. Water.

+ Identity: Anatomy — head. Cultural References. Duality. Numbers — 1.

+ Imagination: Architecture, windows. Astronomy. Color — bright yellow. The Leap. Steps and Stairs.

+ Innocence: Color — white, blue. Crosses. Water — pure.

+ Intelligence: Anatomy — head. Astronomy. Color — clear yellow. Cultural References. Duality. Fire — mind. Numbers. Steps and Stairs.

+ Jealousy: Color — yellow, green. Duality. Fire.

+ Loneliness: Composition. Crosses. Earth — open, empty. Numbers — 0, 1.

+ Love — Anatomy — heart. Color — red. Crosses. Duality. Fire. The Leap. Numbers — 2. Water.

+ Loyalty: Animals — dog. Color — red, blue. Crosses. Cultural References. Numbers — 2.

+ Lust: Anatomy — sex organs. Color — red. Fire. The Leap. Numbers — 2.

+ Memory: Architecture — windows, mirrors. Cultural References. Duality. Step and Stairs.

+ Nurturing: Anatomy — breasts. Color — green, brown. Earth — fertile, rich. Water.

+ Passion: Anatomy — heart, mouth. Color — red. Fire. The Leap. Numbers — 2.

+ Pride: Animals — alpha male. Color — gold, silver, metallics. Cultural References.

+ Sad: Color — blue, gray, washed out. Crosses. Numbers — 1. Step and Stairs — down. Water — rain.

+ Scared — Anatomy — clenched hands, wide-open eyes.

+ Sensuousness: Anatomy — sex organs, legs, feet, hair, eyes, mouth. Architecture — fan. Clothes. Earth — mud. Fire. Water.

+ Shy: Anatomy — hands, closed. Color — gray, black. Numbers — 0.

+ Silly: Animals — goose.

+ Snobbish — Anatomy — hands, closed. Cultural References.

+ Strength: Anatomy — arms. Earth — rocks, mountains. Fire.

+ Unease: Anatomy — distorted. Duality. Water — troubled, storms.

SITUATIONS

+ Alienation: Astronomy. Codes. Crosses. Cultural References (not understood). Duality. Numbers — 1.

+ Barriers: Architecture — fences, walls. Codes. Cultural References. Duality. Fire.

+ Calm: Air. Color — pastels, brown. Earth — fertile, meadows. Water.

+ Challenges: Architecture — fences, walls. Cultural References. Duality. The Leap. Steps and Stairs.

+ Conflict: Duality. Fire. The Leap. Numbers — 2.

✦ Connections: Anatomy — hands. Architecture — bridges. Codes. Crosses. Cultural References. Duality. The Leap (to make them). Numbers — 2. Steps and Stairs. Water.

✦ Danger: Air — storms. Codes. Color — red, black. Crosses. Fire. The Leap.

✦ Death: Anatomy — corpse. Color — black, gray, cold blue. Crosses. Earth — caves, graves. Fire. The Leap. Numbers — 0. Steps and Stairs. Water.

✦ Extinction: Animals — dodo, dinosaur. Color — black. Crosses. Cultural References (not understood). Fire. The Leap. Numbers — 0. Steps and Stairs — down. Water — floods.

✦ Fantasy and Exotic: Animals — dragon, unicorn. Astronomy — stars. Cultural References. The Leap.

✦ Hopeless, Pathetic: Animals — caged animal. Color — washed out. Crosses. Steps and Stairs — down.

✦ Imprisonment: Animals — caged animal. Architecture — towers. Codes. Crosses. Cultural References. Earth — caves. Fire. Water — drowning.

✦ Incorrectness: Anatomy — distorted. Duality.

✦ Movement: Air — wind. Anatomy — legs. The Leap. Water — rushing.

✦ New Life, New Beginnings: Anatomy — sex organs, babies. Animals — egg, babies. Crosses — Christian. Earth — fertile. Fire (purification). The Leap. Numbers — 3, 7. Steps and Stairs. Water.

✦ Oppression: Architecture — low ceilings. Codes. Color — fresh green. Crosses. Cultural References. Earth — barren. Fire — heat. Water — heavy rain.

✦ Poverty: Architecture — huts, shanties. Color — black, brown, gray, muted. Earth — barren. Numbers — 0. Steps and Stairs — down.

✦ Prosperity: Architecture — mansions, palaces, skyscrapers. Color — gold, silver, green, bright. Earth — fertile, expansive. Steps and Stairs — up. Water.

✦ Protection: Anatomy — arms. Codes. Crosses (against evil). Cultural References.

✦ Secrecy: Architecture — walls, fences, blocked windows, covered or cloudy mirrors. Codes. Color — black. Cultural References. Duality. Water — depths.

✦ Separation: Architecture — fences, walls. Codes. Crosses. Cultural References. Duality. The Leap. Numbers — 2. Steps and Stairs.

✦ Sex: Anatomy — sex organs, feet, hair, mouth. Clothes. Color — red, pink. Duality. Fire. The Leap. Numbers — 2. Water.

+ Space (off earth): Astronomy. Color — deep blue, black, twinkling gold and white. The Leap. Steps and Stairs.

+ Spying: Architecture — windows, mirrors. Codes. Color — black. Cultural References. Duality.

+ Status: Architecture. Clothes. Color — purple, jewel tones. Cultural References. Earth (property). Steps and Stairs.

+ Unrest: Air — wind. Duality. Fire. The Leap. Water — turbulent.

CONCEPTS

+ Antiquity, the Past: Architecture — old structures. Astronomy. Chakras. Codes. Earth. Color — faded, gray, brown. Cultural References. Water — undersea cities.

+ Aspiration: Air. Architecture — lofty ceilings, towers. Crosses. Cultural References. The Leap. Steps and Stairs.

+ Balance: Composition. Crosses. Numbers — 2. Water — calm.

+ Capability: Anatomy — hands. Earth — fruitful, agriculture.

+ Consciousness: Anatomy — head. Chakras. Color — yellow. Fire. Numbers — 3, 7. Steps and Stairs.

+ Creativity: Architecture — lofty arches, oversized rooms. Color — yellow. Fire. Steps and Stairs.

+ Doom: Color — gray, black. Crosses. Earth. Fire. The Leap. Numbers — 0. Steps and Stairs — down.

+ Evil: Animals — fierce packs, snakes, predators. Color — red, black. Crosses (protection against). Fire. Numbers — 13.

+ Freedom: Air. Animals — bird. Color — blue. Fire — purification, transfiguration. The Leap. Steps and Stairs.

+ Heaven: Air. Animals — bird. The Leap. Numbers — 7. Steps and Stairs.

+ Hell: Animals — serpents, insects, predators. Earth. Fire. The Leap. Numbers — 0. Steps and Stairs — down.

+ Hope: Air. Color — blue. The Leap. Steps and Stairs.

+ Ideas: Anatomy — head. Codes. Color — yellow. Fire — mind. Steps and Stairs.

+ Independence: Animals — cat. The Leap. Numbers — 1.

+ Loyalty: Animals — dog. Color — red, blue. Cultural References. Earth — rocks. Numbers — 2.

+ Magical, Mystical: Animals — unicorn, dragon. Chakras. Color — purple. Crosses. The Leap. Numbers — 0, 3, 7, 10, 12, 22, 33, 42, 52, 72. Steps and Stairs.

+ Metaphysical: Chakras — Ajna, Crown. Color — purple. Crosses. The Leap. Numbers — 0, 3, 7, 10, 12, 22, 33, 42, 52, 72. Steps and Stairs.

✦ Mockery — Cultural References.

✦ Nature: Air. Animals. Color — green, blue. Earth.

✦ New Age: Astronomy and Astrology. Chakras. Color — purple. Numbers — 0, 3, 7, 10, 12, 22, 33, 42, 52, 72. Steps and Stairs.

✦ Peace: Air. Color — soft. Earth — meadows, fertile. Water — calm.

✦ Perception: Anatomy — eyes, ears. Architecture — windows.

✦ Power: Architecture — oversized lofty rooms, skyscrapers, palaces, domes and rotundas. Color — bold. Cultural References. Earth — mountains, cliffs, rocks. Fire. Steps and Stairs. Water — falls, storms.

✦ Psychic abilities: Anatomy — eyes, ears. Architecture — windows, mirrors. Chakras. Color — purple. The Leap. Numbers — 3, 7, 12, 13, 33, 72. Steps and Stairs. Water.

✦ Sacrifice — Anatomy — heart, blood. Color — red. Crosses. Fire. The Leap. Steps and Stairs — down.

✦ Security and Safety: Air — calm. Architecture — sturdy enclosures. Color — brown, blue. Crosses. Cultural References.

✦ Soul: Animals — bird, egg. Color — blue. Crosses. Numbers — 3, 5, 7. Steps and Stairs. Water.

✦ Speech: Anatomy — mouth.

✦ Spirit, Deity: Air. Animals — bird, egg. Color — white. Fire. The Leap. Numbers — 1, 3. Steps and Stairs.

✦ Transitions: Anatomy — canals, ducts. Architecture — bridges, doors, tunnels, chutes, fans. Chakras. Clothes. Composition. Crosses. Cultural References (from not understood to understood). Fire — transfiguration. The Leap. Numbers — 2, 3, 7. Steps and Stairs. Water.

✦ War: Air — storms. Codes. Color — red, bold, corrupted, rusty. Crosses. Cultural References. Earth — embattled. Fire. The Leap.

BIBLIOGRAPHY

Adkinson, Robert. *Sacred Symbols: A Visual Tour of World Faith.* Abrams, 2009.

Albers, Joseph. *Interaction of Color.* Yale University Press, 1975. Other books by and about Albers.

Arnheim, Rudolf. *Art and Visual Perception: A Psychology of the Creative Eye.* University of California Press, 1974.

Baily, Alice. *The Labors of Hercules: An Astrological Interpretation.* Lucis Publishing Company, 2000.

Bayley, Harold. *The Lost Language of Symbolism.* Volumes I & II. Citadel Press.

Berger, John. *Ways of Seeing.* Penguin, 1990. *About Looking.* Vintage, 1992.

Binder, Pearl. *Magic Symbols of the World.* Hamlyn, 1972.

Block, Bruce. *The Visual Story.* Focal Press, 2001.

Brown, Dan. *Angels & Demons.* Washington Square Press 2006. *The Da Vinci Code.* Anchor, 2009. *The Lost Symbol.* Doubleday Books, 2009.

Bruce-Mitford, Miranda. *Illustrated Book of Signs and Symbols.* DK ADULT, 1996.

Cirlot, J.E. *A Dictionary of Symbols.* Philosophical Library, New York, 1971.

De Lubicz, Schwaller. *Symbol and the Symbolic: Ancient Egypt, Science, and the Evolution of Consciousness.* Inner Traditions, 1981. All his other books.

Dutton, Dennis. *The Art Instinct: Beauty, Pleasure, and Human Evolution.* Bloomsbury, 2008.

Fontana, David. *The Secret Language of Symbols.* Chronicle Books, 1993.

Frazer, James Sir. *The Golden Bough.* This book comes in many versions, from the paperback to the 12-volume series.

Fuller, R. Buckminster. *Critical Path.* St. Martin's Griffin, 1982.

Giannetti, Louis. *Understanding Movies, 11th Edition.* Prentice Hall, 2007.

Hall, Manly P. *Man, Grand Symbol of the Mysteries.* Kessinger Publishing, LLC, 2004.

Hofstadter, Douglas R. *Metamatical Themas: Questing for the Essence of Mind and Pattern.* Basic Books, Inc., New York, 1985.

Holiday, F.W. *The Dragon and the Disk: An Investigation of the Totally Fantastic.* W.W. Norton & Co., Inc., 1973.

Janson, H.W. *History of Art.* Prentice Hall, 1970.

Jung, Carl. *Man and His Symbols.* Doubleday, 1969. *Psyche and Symbol.* Princeton University Press, 1991.

Kandinsky, Wassily. *Concerning the Spiritual in Art.* Dover Publications, 1977. *Point and Line to Plane.* Dover Publications, 1979.

Plongeon, Augustus Le. *Mexican and Egyptian Pyramids.* All his books.

Purce, Jill. *The Mystic Spiral, Journey of the Soul.* Thames and Hudson, 1974.

Ramachandran, V.S., MD, PhD. Many works on art and perception.

Roob, Alexander. *Alchemy and Mysticism.* Taschen, 2001.

Seger, Linda, Dr. *Web Thinking: Connecting, not Competing, for Success.* Inner Ocean Publishing, 2002.

Smith, Pamela Jaye. *INNER DRIVES: Create Characters Using the 8 Centers of Motivation.* Michael Wiese Productions, 2005. *The Power of the Dark Side: Create Great Villains and Dangerous Situations.* Michael Wiese Productions, 2005. *Beyond the Hero's Journey: Other Powerful Mythic Themes.* MYTHWORKS, 1999.

West, John Anthony. *Serpent in the Sky: The Higher Wisdom of Ancient Egypt.* Quest Books, 1993.

Whitley, Dr. David S. *Cave Paintings and the Human Spirit, the Origins of Creativity and Belief.* Prometheus Books, 2009.

Zimmer, Heinrich. Edited by Joseph Campbell. *Myths and Symbols in Indian Art and Civilization.* Princeton University Press, 1974.

DVDS

How Art Made the World. BBC Warner, 2006.

The Great Work. www.thegreatnetwork.org.

Magical Egypt. www.magicalegypt.com.

WEBSITES

Alpha Babe Academy, *www.alphababeacademy.com.*

Bridge Arts Media, *www.bridgeartsmedia.com.*

Caroline Davies, *www.carolinedavies.com.*

Darryl Sapien, *www.sapienfinearts.com.*

Georgia Lambert, *www.Lambert'slodge.com.*

Lodge Intrepid – Men and Women in Freemasonry, *http://lodgeintrepid.org/Home_Page.html*

MYTHWORKS, *www.mythworks.net.*

Philosophical Research Society — Symbolic Art, *http://www.prs.org/gallery.htm.*

Universal Freemasonry — Via Lucis, *http://groups.yahoo.com/group/UFVL/.*

ABOUT THE AUTHOR

photo by Kate McCallum

Pamela Jaye Smith grew up in a world where symbols were essential to livelihood — a cattle ranch in Texas where brands established ownership. Fairy tales, with their exquisitely rich symbolism, filled her childhood. Early years as a Catholic steeped her in the symbolism of that religion, and a lifelong interest in philosophy, history, anthropology, and meta-physics led to eight years of formal classes in Comparative Mysticism. School courses in music, math, and science were filled with the languages of unique notations understood around the world.

At the University of Texas, where she took a BA in English and Latin, with secondary studies in Film, Pamela also studied Buddhism with renowned author and professor Raja Rao. In Los Angeles she studied the physics of metaphysics with Georgia Lambert. Pamela is a Master Mason in a coed Lodge. She was a member of the Advanced Warfighting Working Group at Fort Knox and brought the symbolism of warrior archetypes to seminars there.

Pamela's clients and credits include Microsoft, Disney, Paramount, Universal, RAI-TV Rome, UCLA, USC Film School, American Film Institute, Thot Fiction Marseille France, Natl. Film Institute of Denmark, Pepperdine University, and many more. She has also taught at the Philosophical Research Society and StoryCon: the Art and Science of Story. She is a member of the Institute for Global Transformation and serves on the Advisory Board of the Center for Conscious Creativity. Pamela is the founder of MYTHWORKS: Applied Mythology for More Powerful Reality (*www.mythworks.net*). She is a co-founder of the Alpha Babe Academy (*www.alphababeacademy.com*).

Traveling the world for work and pleasure, Pamela relishes learn-ing about diverse cultures through their stories and symbols. She believes that our experiences of the world are rich and complex with multilayered meanings and that it is the privilege and honor of storytellers and media makers to both create and interpret those meanings for ourselves and others.

MYTHiC TOOLS™

TO HELP YOU IMPROVE YOUR CREATIVITY AND YOUR CRAFT

BOOKS

BEYOND THE HERO'S JOURNEY: Other Powerful Mythic Themes

INNER DRIVES: Create Characters Using the 8 Classic Centers of Motivation (chakras) [*]

PITCHING TIPS FROM ANCIENT AUTHORS

THE POWER OF THE DARK SIDE: Creating Great Villains and Dangerous Situations [*]

CDs

ALPHA BABES, ARCHEPATHS, BEYOND THE HERO'S JOURNEY, CREATING OUR NEXT MYTHS,

WARRIOR WAY FOR FILMMAKERS, and many more

Products available from: MYTHWORKS *www.mythworks.net* / The Writers Store *www.writersstore.com*

*[*Also at Amazon and your local bookstore.]*

STORY CONSULTATIONS, SPEAKER, TEACHER

Pamela Jaye Smith *www.pamelajayesmith.com* *pjs@pamelajayesmith.com* 323-874-6447

ALPHA BABE ACADEMY

www.alphababeacademy.com

INNER DRIVES
HOW TO WRITE AND CREATE CHARACTERS USING THE EIGHT CLASSIC CENTERS OF MOTIVATION

PAMELA JAYE SMITH

Inspiring and practical, *Inner Drives* goes to the very source of character motivation and action. Exploring the fascinating world of archetypes, mythology, and the chakra system, writers will learn to apply timeless principles of successful storytelling through fascinating examples and valuable exercises.

From patterns of speech to styles of walking, writers can use Pamela Jaye Smith's guide to structure character arcs, devise backstories, up the conflict, pair up couples, and form ensembles — all with unique, believable characters.

Informative and entertaining, this book helps writers, directors, designers, development executives, and actors expand their artistry and influence on the audience to gain a creative advantage in a highly competitive industry.

"In *Inner Drives*, Pamela Jaye Smith has created a masterpiece that magically combines myth with motivation, the use of chakras in the craft of writing, and self-exploration as an integral part of storytelling. Whether you are writing your masterpiece, or just trying to better understand yourself and those you interact with, *Inner Drives* will give you the intimate intricate detail you need to grasp the universal realities of Planet Hollywood, and indeed of Planet Earth."
— Lynn Santer, Author, *Sins of Life*, *Into the Fire*, *Evil by Design*; Filmmaker, *Lewis's Piano*

"Pamela Jaye Smith's *Inner Drives* is written for screenwriters, but will be welcomed by everyone from novelists to TV sitcom writers. It explores what makes a character tick, the choices one person may make compared to another, and the deep structure of character. Highly readable with plenty of story examples, this wonderful book will make new or experienced writers very happy."
— Mollie Gregory, Author, *Women Who Run the Show - How A New Generation Stormed Hollywood*, *Making Films Your Business*, *Triplets*, *Birthstone*, *Privileged Lies*

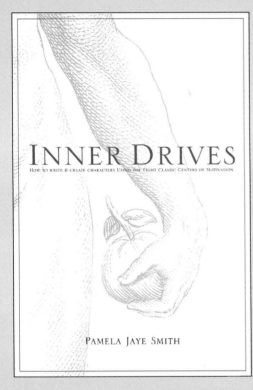

PAMELA JAYE SMITH is a writer, mythologist, consultant, speaker, and award-winning producer/director with international clients and credits in features, TV, commercials, music videos, documentaries, and corporate films.

$26.95 | 264 PAGES | ORDER NUMBER 32RLS | ISBN: 9781932907032

THE POWER OF THE DARK SIDE
CREATING GREAT VILLAINS AND DANGEROUS SITUATIONS

PAMELA JAYE SMITH

Who doesn't love the Dark Side? Darth Vader, Cruella De Vil, Tony Soprano — everybody loves a great villain. And every story needs dramatic conflict — internal and external — to really resonate. This comprehensive, accessible book gives you tools to craft the most despicable villains in your stories.

Conflict is the very heart and soul of drama. Mythologist Pamela Jaye Smith's latest book explores character conflict and a multitude of ways to achieve it:

· Defining the Dark Side helps you select and clarify the worldview that influences your characters' actions.

· The Three Levels of the Dark Side — personal, impersonal, and supra-personal — offer layers of interweaving conflict.

· A roll-call of Villains includes Profiles and Suggestions for creating your own versions of reader's bad-to-the-bone favorites.

· Learn to match Antagonists to Protagonists, and to use the Sliding Scale of Evil.

"The Power of the Dark Side *is an incredible exploration of the different dimensions of Evil. Pamela Jaye Smith demonstrates once again that she is one of the world's experts, not only on multicultural mythology but also on the application of the ideas of archetype, symbol, and cognitive science. While she's written this book with the writer in mind, her exploration of the ideas of evil will be of great value to teachers, therapists, and anyone who deals with people, education, motivation, or persuasion. For writers, it opens up a world of ideas that will help in building more complex antagonists. To have a great hero, you need a great villain.* Dark Side *delivers far more than you'd expect from one book.*"

— Rob Kall, publisher of *OpEdNews.com* and founder, Storycon Summit Meeting on the Art, Science and Application of Story

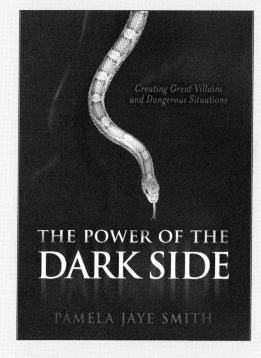

PAMELA JAYE SMITH is an international speaker, consultant, writer, award-winning producer-director, and founder of MYTHWORKS *www.mythworks.net.* Credits include Microsoft, Paramount, Disney, Universal, GM, Boeing, the FBI and US Army. Smith has authored the MWP book, *Inner Drives.* She has taught writers, directors, and actors at USC, UCLA, American Film Institute, RAI-TV Rome, Denmark, France, New Zealand, Brazil, and many other venues.

$22.95 | 266 PAGES | ORDER NUMBER 82RLS | ISBN: 9781932907438

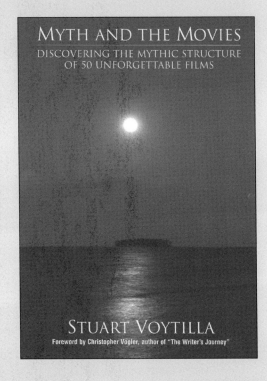

STEALING FIRE FROM THE GODS
2ND EDITION
THE COMPLETE GUIDE TO STORY
FOR WRITERS & FILMMAKERS

JAMES BONNET

Unlocking the secrets of story reveals the secrets of the mind and awakens the power of story within you. Work with that power and you can steal fire from the gods. Master that power and you can create stories that will live forever.

James Bonnet gives you the principles and tools you need to create motion pictures packed with emotion, mega-hits that will resonate for generations. He will teach you:

- How to emulate the natural creative story-making process and put all of your conscious and un-conscious creative powers into your work

- The nature and purpose of story, the compass that will orient you toward the real needs and desires of the audience

- How to use the creative process, the language of metaphor, and a sophisticated story model to bring powerful hidden truths to the surface — all without compromising in any way the things you really want to write about

- How to dramatically transform your own and other people's lives

This revised and expanded second edition includes important new revelations concerning the ultimate source of unity, the structures of the whole story passage, the anti-hero's journey, the high-concept great idea, the secrets of charismatic characters, and the analysis of many important new stories and successful films.

"Anyone who is interested in structuring feelings and thought into words and story will find Stealing Fire *stimulating and worthwhile. A lifetime's labor of love, it provides the reader with insight, and an overview of the creative process through the history of story. I recommend it highly."*

> — Elliott Gould, Actor,
> Academy Award® Nominee

JAMES BONNET, founder of *storymaking.com*, is an internationally known writer, teacher, and story consultant.

CINEMATIC STORYTELLING
THE 100 MOST POWERFUL FILM
CONVENTIONS EVERY FILMMAKER MUST KNOW

JENNIFER VAN SIJL

BEST SELLER

How do directors use screen direction to suggest conflict? How do screenwriters exploit film space to show change? How does editing style determine emotional response?

Many first-time writers and directors do not ask these questions. They forego the huge creative resource of the film medium, defaulting to dialog to tell their screen story. Yet most movies are carried by sound and picture. The industry's most successful writers and directors have mastered the cinematic conventions specific to the medium. They have harnessed non-dialog techniques to create some of the most cinematic moments in movie history.

This book is intended to help writers and directors more fully exploit the medium's inherent storytelling devices. It contains 100 non-dialog techniques that have been used by the industry's top writers and directors. From *Metropolis* and *Citizen Kane* to *Dead Man* and *Kill Bill*,

the book illustrates — through 500 frame grabs and 75 script excerpts — how the inherent storytelling devices specific to film were exploited.

You will learn:
- · How non-dialog film techniques can advance story.
- · How master screenwriters exploit cinematic conventions to create powerful scenarios.

"*Cinematic Storytelling scores a direct hit in terms of concise information and perfectly chosen visuals, and it also searches out... and finds... an emotional core that many books of this nature either miss or are afraid of.*"

— Kirsten Sheridan, Director,
Disco Pigs; Co-writer, *In America*

"*Here is a uniquely fresh, accessible, and truly original contribution to the field. Jennifer van Sijll takes her readers in a wholly new direction, integrating aspects of screenwriting with all the film crafts in a way I've never before seen. It is essential reading not only for screenwriters but also for filmmakers of every stripe.*"

— Prof. Richard Walter,
UCLA Screenwriting Chairman

JENNIFER VAN SIJLL has taught film production, film history, and screenwriting. She is currently on the faculty at San Francisco State's Department of Cinema.

$24.95 | 230 PAGES | ORDER NUMBER 35RLS | ISBN: 9781932907056

SAVE THE CAT!®
GOES TO THE MOVIES
THE SCREENWRITER'S GUIDE TO EVERY STORY EVER TOLD

BLAKE SNYDER

BEST SELLER

In the long-awaited sequel to his surprise bestseller, *Save the Cat!*, author and screenwriter Blake Snyder returns to form in a fast-paced follow-up that proves why his is the most talked-about approach to screenwriting in years. In the perfect companion piece to his first book, Snyder delivers even more insider's information gleaned from a 20-year track record as "one of Hollywood's most successful spec screenwriters," giving you the clues to write *your* movie.

Designed for screenwriters, novelists, and movie fans, this book gives readers the key breakdowns of the 50 most instructional movies from the past 30 years. From *M*A*S*H* to *Crash*, from *Alien* to *Saw*, from *10* to *Eternal Sunshine of the Spotless Mind*, Snyder reveals how screenwriters who came before you tackled the same challenges you are facing with the film you want to write — or the one you are currently working on.

If you want to sell your script and create a movie that pleases most audiences most of the time, the odds increase if you reference Snyder's checklists and see what makes 50 films tick. After all, both executives and audiences respond to the same elements good writers seek to master. They want to know the type of story they signed on for, and whether it's structured in a way that satisfies everyone. It's what they're looking for. And now, it's what you can deliver.

"*Blake has done it again!* Save the Cat! Goes to the Movies *puts his easy-to-digest theories to the test and proves them time after time. With great insight and wit, Blake has identified the key components of good storytelling and presented them in a clear, indisputable form that is at once universal and immediately applicable... no matter where you are in the writing process. Blake is a light-switch in the dank, cluttered basement of story. What an eye-opener.*"

— Dean DeBlois, Co-Writer/Director,
Lilo & Stitch

"*You can't think outside the box until you understand what it is — and nobody understands the box that movies come in the way Blake does. A fantastic book!*"

— Jeff Arch, Writer, *Sleepless in Seattle*
(Oscar®-nominated), *Saving Milly*

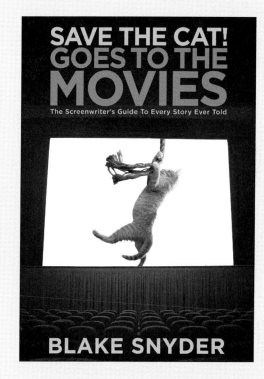

BLAKE SNYDER, besides selling million-dollar scripts to both Disney and Spielberg, was one of Hollywood's most successful spec screenwriters. Blake's vision continues on *www.blakesnyder.com*.

$24.95 | 270 PAGES | ORDER NUMBER 75RLS | ISBN: 9781932907353

THE HOLLYWOOD STANDARD
2ND EDITION
THE COMPLETE AND AUTHORITATIVE GUIDE TO SCRIPT FORMAT AND STYLE

CHRISTOPHER RILEY

BEST SELLER

This is the book screenwriter Antwone Fisher (*Antwone Fisher*, *Tales from the Script*) insists his writing students at UCLA read. This book convinced John August (*Big Fish*, *Charlie and the Chocolate Factory*) to stop dispensing formatting advice on his popular writing website. His new advice: Consult *The Hollywood Standard*. The book working and aspiring writers keep beside their keyboards and rely on every day. Written by a professional screenwriter whose day job was running the vaunted script shop at Warner Bros., this book is used at USC's School of Cinema, UCLA, and the acclaimed Act One Writing Program in Hollywood, and in screenwriting programs around the world. It is the definitive guide to script format.

The *Hollywood Standard* describes in clear, vivid prose and hundreds of examples how to format every element of a screenplay or television script. A reference for everyone who writes for the screen, from the novice to the veteran, this is the dictionary of script format, with instructions for formatting everything from the simplest master scene heading to the most complex and challenging musical underwater dream sequence. This new edition includes a quick start guide, plus new chapters on avoiding a dozen deadly formatting mistakes, clarifying the difference between a spec script and production script, and mastering the vital art of proofreading. For the first time, readers will find instructions for formatting instant messages, text messages, email exchanges and caller ID.

"Aspiring writers sometimes wonder why people don't want to read their scripts. Sometimes it's not their story. Sometimes the format distracts. To write a screenplay, you need to learn the science. And this is the best, simplest, easiest to read book to teach you that science. It's the one I recommend to my students at UCLA."

— Antwone Fisher, from the foreword

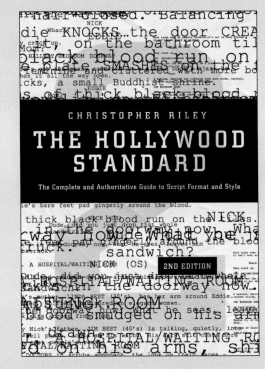

CHRISTOPHER RILEY is a professional screenwriter working in Hollywood with his wife and writing partner, Kathleen Riley. Together they wrote the 1999 theatrical feature *After the Truth*, a multiple-award-winning German language courtroom thriller.

$24.95 | 208 PAGES | ORDER NUMBER 130RLS | ISBN: 9781932907636

THE MYTH OF MWP

In a dark time, a light bringer came along, leading the curious and the frustrated to clarity and empowerment. It took the well-guarded secrets out of the hands of the few and made them available to all. It spread a spirit of openness and creative freedom, and built a storehouse of knowledge dedicated to the betterment of the arts.

The essence of the Michael Wiese Productions (MWP) is empowering people who have the burning desire to express themselves creatively. We help them realize their dreams by putting the tools in their hands. We demystify the sometimes secretive worlds of screenwriting, directing, acting, producing, film financing, and other media crafts.

By doing so, we hope to bring forth a realization of 'conscious media' which we define as being positively charged, emphasizing hope and affirming positive values like trust, cooperation, self-empowerment, freedom, and love. Grounded in the deep roots of myth, it aims to be healing both for those who make the art and those who encounter it. It hopes to be transformative for people, opening doors to new possibilities and pulling back veils to reveal hidden worlds.

MWP has built a storehouse of knowledge unequaled in the world, for no other publisher has so many titles on the media arts. Please visit www.mwp.com where you will find many free resources and a 25% discount on our books. Sign up and become part of the wider creative community!

Onward and upward,

Michael Wiese
Publisher/Filmmaker

FILM & VIDEO BOOKS
TO RECEIVE A FREE MWP NEWSLETTER, CLICK ON WWW.MWP.COM TO REGISTER

SCREENWRITING | WRITING

And the Best Screenplay Goes to... | Dr. Linda Seger | $26.95

Archetypes for Writers | Jennifer Van Bergen | $22.95

Bali Brothers | Lacy Waltzman, Matthew Bishop, Michael Wiese | $12.95

Cinematic Storytelling | Jennifer Van Sijll | $24.95

Could It Be a Movie? | Christina Hamlett | $26.95

Creating Characters | Marisa D'Vari | $26.95

Crime Writer's Reference Guide, The | Martin Roth | $20.95

Deep Cinema | Mary Trainor-Brigham | $19.95

Elephant Bucks | Sheldon Bull | $24.95

Fast, Cheap & Written That Way | John Gaspard | $26.95

Hollywood Standard, The, 2nd Edition | Christopher Riley | $18.95

Horror Screenwriting | Devin Watson | $24.95

I Could've Written a Better Movie than That! | Derek Rydall | $26.95

Inner Drives | Pamela Jaye Smith | $26.95

Moral Premise, The | Stanley D. Williams, Ph.D. | $24.95

Myth and the Movies | Stuart Voytilla | $26.95

Power of the Dark Side, The | Pamela Jaye Smith | $22.95

Psychology for Screenwriters | William Indick, Ph.D. | $26.95

Reflections of the Shadow | Jeffrey Hirschberg | $26.95

Rewrite | Paul Chitlik | $16.95

Romancing the A-List | Christopher Keane | $18.95

Save the Cat! | Blake Snyder | $19.95

Save the Cat! Goes to the Movies | Blake Snyder | $24.95

Screenwriting 101 | Neill D. Hicks | $16.95

Screenwriting for Teens | Christina Hamlett | $18.95

Script-Selling Game, The | Kathie Fong Yoneda | $16.95

Stealing Fire From the Gods, 2nd Edition | James Bonnet | $26.95

Talk the Talk | Penny Penniston | $24.95

Way of Story, The | Catherine Ann Jones | $22.95

What Are You Laughing At? | Brad Schreiber | $19.95

Writer's Journey, – 3rd Edition, The | Christopher Vogler | $26.95

Writer's Partner, The | Martin Roth | $24.95

Writing the Action Adventure Film | Neill D. Hicks | $14.95

Writing the Comedy Film | Stuart Voytilla & Scott Petri | $14.95

Writing the Killer Treatment | Michael Halperin | $14.95

Writing the Second Act | Michael Halperin | $19.95

Writing the Thriller Film | Neill D. Hicks | $14.95

Writing the TV Drama Series – 2nd Edition | Pamela Douglas | $26.95

Your Screenplay Sucks! | William M. Akers | $19.95

FILMMAKING

Film School | Richard D. Pepperman | $24.95

Power of Film, The | Howard Suber | $27.95

PITCHING

Perfect Pitch – 2nd Edition, The | Ken Rotcop | $19.95

Selling Your Story in 60 Seconds | Michael Hauge | $12.95

SHORTS

Filmmaking for Teens, 2nd Edition | Troy Lanier & Clay Nichols | $24.95

Making It Big in Shorts | Kim Adelman | $22.95

BUDGET | PRODUCTION MANAGEMENT

Film & Video Budgets, 5th Updated Edition | Deke Simon | $26.95

Film Production Management 101 | Deborah S. Patz | $39.95

DIRECTING | VISUALIZATION

Animation Unleashed | Ellen Besen | $26.95

Cinematography for Directors | Jacqueline Frost | $29.95

Citizen Kane Crash Course in Cinematography | David Worth | $19.95

Directing Actors | Judith Weston | $26.95

Directing Feature Films | Mark Travis | $26.95

Fast, Cheap & Under Control | John Gaspard | $26.95

Film Directing: Cinematic Motion, 2nd Edition | Steven D. Katz | $27.95

Film Directing: Shot by Shot | Steven D. Katz | $27.95

Film Director's Intuition, The | Judith Weston | $26.95

First Time Director | Gil Bettman | $27.95

From Word to Image, 2nd Edition | Marcie Begleiter | $26.95

I'll Be in My Trailer! | John Badham & Craig Modderno | $26.95

Master Shots | Christopher Kenworthy | $24.95

Setting Up Your Scenes | Richard D. Pepperman | $24.95

Setting Up Your Shots, 2nd Edition | Jeremy Vineyard | $22.95

Working Director, The | Charles Wilkinson | $22.95

DIGITAL | DOCUMENTARY | SPECIAL

Digital Filmmaking 101, 2nd Edition | Dale Newton & John Gaspard | $26.95

Digital Moviemaking 3.0 | Scott Billups | $24.95

Digital Video Secrets | Tony Levelle | $26.95

Greenscreen Made Easy | Jeremy Hanke & Michele Yamazaki | $19.95

Producing with Passion | Dorothy Fadiman & Tony Levelle | $22.95

Special Effects | Michael Slone | $31.95

EDITING

Cut by Cut | Gael Chandler | $35.95

Cut to the Chase | Bobbie O'Steen | $24.95

Eye is Quicker, The | Richard D. Pepperman | $27.95

Film Editing | Gael Chandler | $34.95

Invisible Cut, The | Bobbie O'Steen | $28.95

SOUND | DVD | CAREER

Complete DVD Book, The | Chris Gore & Paul J. Salamoff | $26.95

Costume Design 101, 2nd Edition | Richard La Motte | $24.95

Hitting Your Mark, 2nd Edition | Steve Carlson | $22.95

Sound Design | David Sonnenschein | $19.95

Sound Effects Bible, The | Ric Viers | $26.95

Storyboarding 101 | James Fraioli | $19.95

There's No Business Like Soul Business | Derek Rydall | $22.95

You Can Act! | D. W. Brown | $24.95

FINANCE | MARKETING | FUNDING

Art of Film Funding, The | Carole Lee Dean | $26.95

Bankroll | Tom Malloy | $26.95

Complete Independent Movie Marketing Handbook, The | Mark Steven Bosko | $39.95

Getting the Money | Jeremy Jusso | $26.95

Independent Film and Videomakers Guide – 2nd Edition, The | Michael Wiese | $29.95

Independent Film Distribution | Phil Hall | $26.95

Shaking the Money Tree, 3rd Edition | Morrie Warshawski | $26.95

MEDITATION | ART

Mandalas of Bali | Dewa Nyoman Batuan | $39.95

OUR FILMS

Dolphin Adventures: DVD | Michael Wiese and Hardy Jones | $24.95

Hardware Wars: DVD | Written and Directed by Ernie Fosselius | $14.95

On the Edge of a Dream | Michael Wiese | $16.95

Sacred Sites of the Dalai Lamas– DVD, The | Documentary by Michael Wiese | $24.95